UNIVERSITY OF WALES SWANSEA
PRIFYSGOL CYMRU ABERTAWE
LIBRARY/LLYFRGELL

Classmark NK1071 ADM STOCK

Location Miners Library.

1004911716

ook must be returned immed-

KU-208-841

The Unknown Craftsman

The Unknown Craftsman

A Japanese Insight into Beauty

Sōetsu Yanagi

Adapted by Bernard Leach

Foreword by Shōji Hamada

KODANSHA INTERNATIONAL
Tokyo • New York • London

Distributed in the United States by Kodansha America, Inc.,
114 Fifth Avenue, New York, N.Y. 10011, and in the United
Kingdom and continental Europe by Kodansha Europe Ltd., 95
Aldwych, London WC2B 4JF. Published by Kodansha Interna-
tional Ltd., 17-14 Otowa 1-chome, Bunkyo-ku, Tokyo 112, and
Kodansha America, Inc.

Copyright © 1972 and 1989 by Kodansha International. Photo-
graphs copyright © 1972 and 1989 by Mingei-kan. All rights
reserved. Printed in Japan.

Original hardcover edition, 1972
First paperback edition, 1978
Fourth printing, 1984
Revised edition, 1989
    97 98 99 10 9 8 7

ISBN 4-7700-1448-1 (Japan)

Library of Congress Cataloging-in-Publication Data

Yanagi, Muneyoshi, 1889–1961.
    The unknown craftsman.

    1. Decoration and ornament—Japan. 2. Design—Japan.
I. Leach, Berhard, 1887– . II. Title.
NK1071.A1Y36 1989   745.4'4952   89-24645
ISBN 0-87011-948-6

UNIVERSITY COLLEGE
LIBRARY
SWANSEA

Contents

In Gratitude 8

Yanagi and Leach   *Shōji Hamada*   9

Plates 11

Introduction   *Bernard Leach*   87

Towards a Standard of Beauty 101

Seeing and Knowing 109

Pattern 113

The Beauty of Irregularity 119

The Buddhist Idea of Beauty 127

Crafts of Okinawa 158

Hakeme 170

The Way of Tea 177

The Kizaemon Tea-bowl 190

The Way of Craftsmanship 197

The Responsibility of the Craftsman 216

Index 225

This book is dedicated to the life and work of my old friend Sōetsu Yanagi.

Sōetsu Yanagi, sketch by Bernard Leach.

In Gratitude

THIS VOLUME HAS TAKEN ten years to conclude. My heartfelt thanks go out to many whose faith and friendship have brought this about.

First, to my Japanese secretary, Hiroshi Mizuo, himself a young author, poet and art historian, who for a time worked with Sōetsu Yanagi at the Japan Folkcraft Museum in Tokyo. He was followed by Miss Sonoe Asakawa, who for many years was Yanagi's private secretary and assistant. With their devoted help a longer book reached typescript stage, only for me to discover through my third helper, Miss Mihoko Okamura—born and educated in New York and therefore whose English was natural—that the script was too much my interpretation of Yanagi to be called a translation. We started all over again. Miss Okamura came twice to Cornwall to work with me. Thanks are due to my wife Janet for her encouragement throughout in what we believe to be a unique contribution to an English-reading public. Now, after such inevitable delays, I sit looking directly across the Atlantic working on the final reading corrections and suggestions with the help of my private secretary Trudi Scott.

To all these, to Toyotarō Tanaka, the staff of the Japan Folkcraft Museum, and many others who have assisted loyally in the prolonged making of this book, I record my profound thanks.—B.L.

Yanagi and Leach

In the autumn of 1964 an international exhibition of contemporary studio pottery was held in Tokyo. Most of the work selected came from Europe, America, and Japan and was "abstract" in character, clearly showing the pressures of present-day life and art.

I felt a general lack of maturity both in motivation and technique. The first impression given was one of power, or force, but it was followed by a sensation of violence and at the same time of emptiness. On the whole, the Japanese exhibits had a greater traditional content and were more skilful in technique, but were less alive than the pots from the West. Shells without fish. The abstract examples were mannered and did not spring from a genuine internal life.

In the whole exhibition, the pots that I admired most were made by Bernard Leach. Many other Japanese potters agreed with me. Curiously, these were the quietest pots in the whole show. Whether he works in the East or the West he preserves a simple and straightforward approach. The focus of his work is the most concentrated and personally expressive. This quality in his work has been apparent for over fifty years. The feeling in his pots comes from a high inspiration that defeats both weakened traditions and the violence of modern motivation I have mentioned. He draws his strength from the soil of his own nature and his life experience. This is spring water. I feel the difference between this inspiration and that of others very strongly. His stance between East and West is a true balance, not a measured middle.

When Sōetsu Yanagi was young, he immersed himself in Christian mysticism. At that stage he wrote a long book on William Blake and published a Japanese magazine called *Blake and Whitman*. Later, together with his literary and painter friends, he entered the world of Post-Impressionism, Impressionism, and so back over the centuries of European art to the Renaissance and to the Primitives. That took him gradually back to his own East, especially to Korean art and to Japanese folk art, which he may be truly said to have discovered. This was not an intellectual and systematic process with him, but one of intuition dictated by an extraordinary visual perception of truth. In like manner, as a religious philosopher and as a disciple and friend of Dr. Daisetsu Suzuki, he searched his way through the developments of Buddhist thought—Zen first, for the lone seeker, followed by Jōdo Shinshū and Jishū for the many, the two aspects called *jiriki* ("Self Power") and *tariki* ("Other Power") respectively. Finally he reached that point where the apparent difference is fused and cancelled out. That led him to the consideration of beauty and ugliness in art and to the need of an aesthetic that embraces both. Thus he arrived at his Kingdom of Beauty.

Yanagi and Leach shared a similarity of approach during fifty years of close friendship, even when they were half a world apart. In fact they were never apart. Yanagi is gone, but the friendship has deepened. Leach has translated a selection of Yanagi's essays in a way that no one else could have done, and this in itself is a creative continuance of that friendship.

What impresses me most in Yanagi is the strength of his vision, his direct eye for beauty. Critics, in general, may be divided into those who collect, and who get bogged down in collecting, and those who split hairs of aesthetics. Yanagi escaped both pitfalls. He employed no intellectual foot-rule. His was an immediate and intuitive faculty of an extraordinary kind. His actions followed fast upon the heels of this perception.

Visitors to the folkcraft museum in Tokyo often complain of the brevity of the descriptions of the objects, written in red on black lacquer tablets, saying that this is inconsiderate and insufficient. Yanagi always insisted that this was a greater kindness because it helped visitors to develop their own perceptions instead of relying upon written words and other people's ideas. All this causes me to describe Yanagi as a creative critic.

Leach's *A Potter's Book* is known in America and elsewhere as a potter's Bible. I have the idea that this present volume will come to be regarded in the future as a sutra of Oriental aesthetics.

Shōji Hamada

1. Kizaemon Ido teabowl. Korea. Yi dynasty (sixteenth century). Height: 8.8 cm.

3. Bottle, iron-glazed stoneware. Korea. Koryo dynasty (thirteenth century). Height: 21 cm.

◁ 2. Kimono detail, warp- and weft-dyed (*kasuri*) silk.
   Okinawa. Eighteenth century.

4. Bowl, brushmarked (*hakeme*) stoneware. Korea. Yi dynasty (seventeenth century).
Diameter: 17.1 cm.

5. Painting from a "Tale of Tsukishima" handscroll. Provenance unknown. Sixteenth century. Width: 32 cm.

7. Kimono detail, stencil-dyed (*bingata*) hemp. ▷
Okinawa. Eighteenth century.

6. Plate, stoneware. Shino type, Mino ware, Gifu Prefecture. Seventeenth century.
Diameter: 24.5 cm.

8. Saké server, gold leaf and lacquer on wood. Northern Honshu. Eighteenth century.
Diameter: 20.5 cm.

9. Salt jar, stoneware with accidental ash glaze. Tamba ware, Hyōgo Prefecture. Seventeenth century. Height: 11 cm.

11. Courtesan, *Ōstu-e* painting. ▷
Ōtsu, Shiga Prefecture. Seventeenth
century. Height: 60 cm.

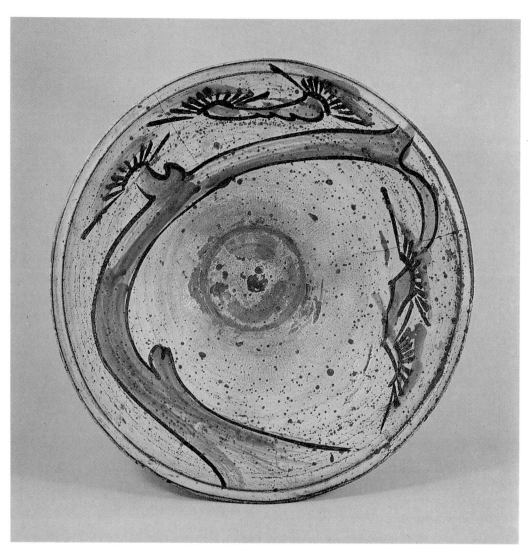

10. Mixing basin, earthenware. Futagawa ware, Saga Prefecture. Eighteenth century.
Diameter: 55 cm.

12. Stationery box, lacquer on wood. Yamagata Prefecture. Eighteenth century. Length: 33 cm.

◁ 13. The Shinto god Tajikara-o-no-Mikoto, stone relief
rubbing. Nagano Prefecture. Nineteenth century. Height:
51.5 cm.

14. Female figurine (back view), stone. Iwate Prefecture. Latest Jōmon period
(*ca.* 1000–250 B.C.). Width: 19 cm.

15. Buddha, gilded stone. Korea. Koryo dynasty (eleventh century). Height: 45 cm.

16. Calligraphy by Sōetsu Yanagi. "Absolute Compassion".

17. Calligraphy by Sōetsu Yanagi. "Don't say tomorrow".

18. Calligraphy by Sōetsu Yanagi. "Today the sky is clear".

19. Calligraphy by Sōetsu Yanagi. "Beyond beauty and ugliness".

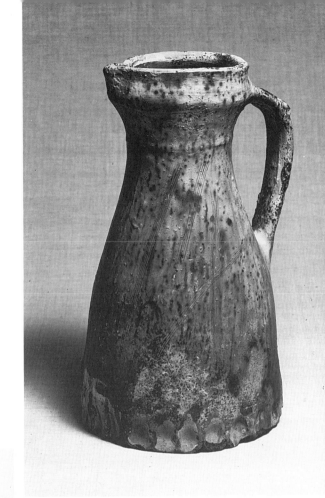

◁ 20. Pitcher, earthenware. England.
Thirteenth century. Height: 45 cm.

21. Pitchers, earthenware. England. Fourteenth
century. Height: above, 26.5 cm.; left, 25.5 cm.

22. Lidded cup, white-glazed earthenware. China. Sung dynasty. Height: 9.5 cm.

23. Family crest with bamboo-grass design. Japan.

24. Townhouse (*above*), Izumo, Shimane Prefecture.
Farmhouse (*right*), Shirakawa-mura, Gifu Prefecture.

25. Small tray, lacquer on wood. Nara Prefecture. Eighteenth century. Diameter: 24.5 cm.

26. Farmer's coat, stitched cotton. Northern Honshu. Nineteenth century. Height: 130 cm.

27. Coptic textile. Egypt. Seventh century. Height: 22.5 cm.

28. Lidded jars, stoneware. Swankolok, Thailand. Fifteenth century.
Heights: left, 10.2 cm.; right, 6.5 cm.

29. Painting "Descending Geese," one of
the Eight Views of Hsiao-Hsiang. Korea.
Yi dynasty. Height: 90 cm.

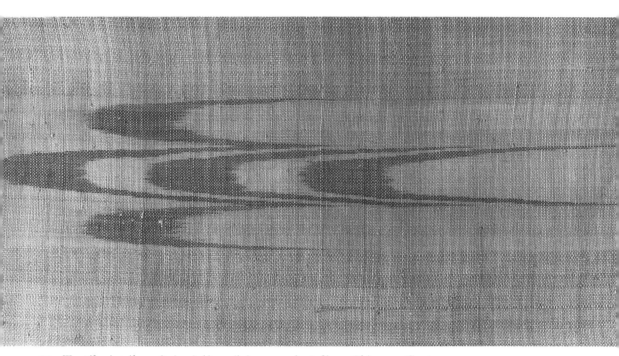

30. Textile detail, weft-dyed (*kasuri*) banana-plant fibre. Okinawa. Contemporary.

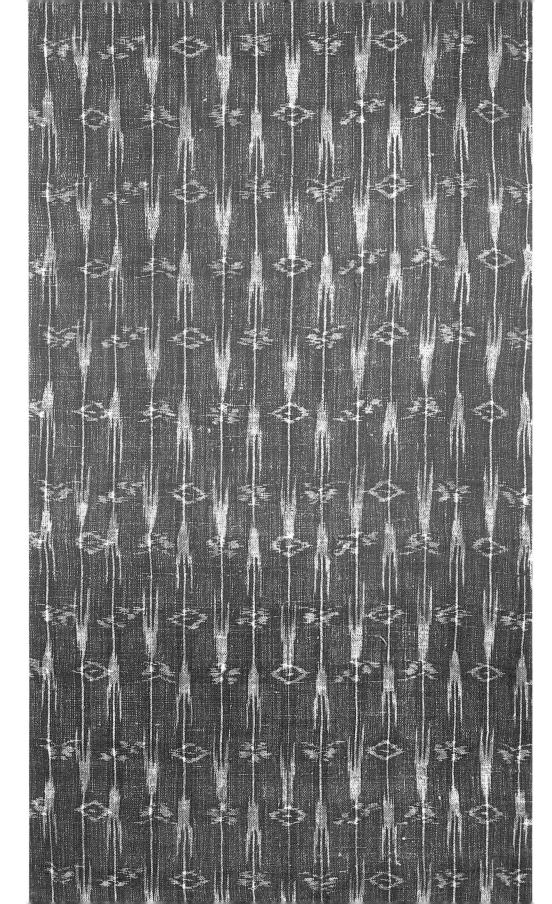

32. Noodle cup (*upper left*) and teacups, porcelain. Imari ware, Saga Prefecture. Nineteenth century. Heights: 5.5 cm.

◁ 31. Textile detail, warp- and weft-dyed (*kasuri*) hemp.
  Ojiya, Niigata Prefecture. Nineteenth century.

33. Toy, papier mâché. Miharu, Fukushima Prefecture. Eighteenth century. Height: 18 cm.

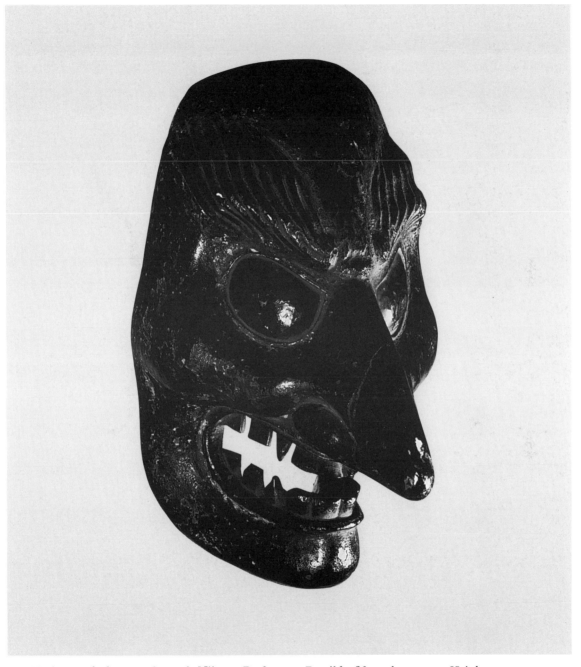

34. Votive mask, lacquered wood. Niigata Prefecture. Possibly fifteenth century. Height: 27 cm.

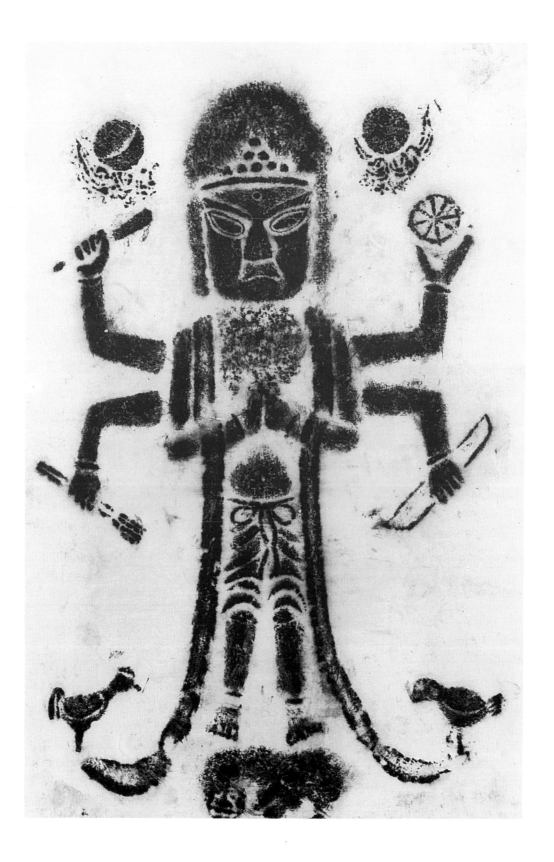

36. Baking dish, earthenware with slip decoration. England. Probably eighteenth century.
Width: 46.5 cm.

◁ 35. Buddhist guardian deity (Kongo), incised stone rubbing.
   Nagano Prefecture. Seventeenth century. Height: 84 cm.

37. High-footed tray, raw-lacquered wood. Korea. Yi dynasty (eighteenth century). Height: 22 cm.

38. Jar, stoneware. Korea. Early Yi dynasty (fifteenth century). Height: 18.5 cm.

39. Coat, woven silk remnants. Fukui Prefecture. Nineteenth century. Height: 130 cm.

40. Rice bowl, lacquer on wood. Northern Honshu. Eighteenth century. Height: 9 cm.

41. Self-portrait sculpture by
Mokujiki Shōnin (1718–1810)
wood. Height: 72 cm.

42. Bodhidharma, *Ōtsu-e* painting.
Ōtsu, Shiga Prefecture. Seventeenth
century. Height: 39.5 cm.

43. Royal tombs, Shuri, Okinawa (prewar photo).

44. Tombs, Okinawa (prewar photo).

45. Shuri, Okinawa (prewar photo).

46. Enkaku-ji temple, Shuri, Okinawa (prewar photo).

47. "Devil" roof tiles, Okinawa (prewar photo).

48. Roof *shishi*, Okinawa (prewar photo).

49. Stencil dyeing (*bingata*) stencil, paper. Okinawa. Modern. Height: 55 cm.

50. Textile detail (*hana'ui* and *kasuri*), banana-plant fibre and cotton. Yomitan, Okinawa.

51. Pottery yard, Tsuboya, Okinawa, with funerary urns drying (prewar photo).

52. Funerary urn, stoneware. Tsuboya, Okinawa. Modern. Height: 48.5 cm.

53. Chopstick stand, stoneware. Tsuboya, Okinawa. Nineteenth century. Height: 14.6 cm.

54. Saké server, stoneware. Tsuboya, Okinawa. Nineteenth century. Height: 11.8 cm.

55. Liquor server, stoneware. Naeshirogawa, Kagoshima Prefecture. Modern. Height: 16 cm.

56. Teapot, stoneware. White Satsuma ware, Kagoshima Prefecture. Nineteenth century. Height: 19 cm.

57. Bowl, semi-porcelain. Korea. Yi dynasty (seventeenth century). Diameter: 11.2 cm.

58. Liquor server, oiled wood. Korea. Yi dynasty (nineteenth century). Height: 12.5 cm.

59. Teabowl, semi-porcelain with white engobe. ▷
Korea. Yi dynasty. Diameter: 15 cm.

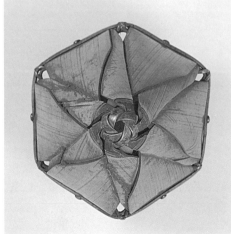

60. Wall-hanging flower container, bamboo. Provenance
unknown. Nineteenth century. Height: 23.7 cm.

61. Box, bamboo with brass fittings. Korea. Yi dynasty. Length: 30 cm.

62. Incense burner, soapstone. Korea. Yi dynasty. Diameter: 28.5 cm.

63. Small desk, wood with brass fittings. Korea. Yi dynasty. Length: 72 cm.

64. Ceremonial stand, porcelain. Korea. Yi dynasty (eighteenth century). Height: 8 cm.

65. Water dropper for inkstone, porcelain. ▷
Korea. Yi dynasty. Length: 8 cm.

66. Water dropper for inkstone, porcelain.
Korea. Yi dynasty. Diameter: 10 cm.

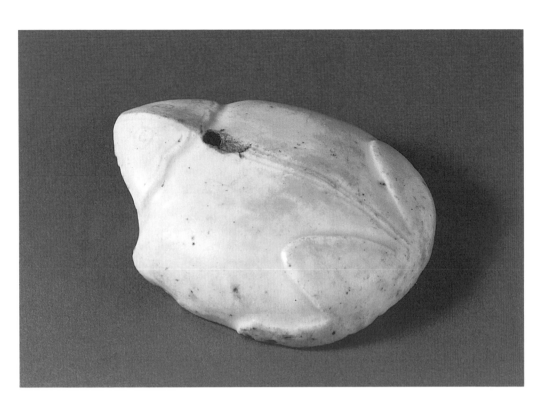

67. Jar, stoneware. Korea. Yi dynasty (seventeenth century). Height: 18.8 cm.

68. Jar, stoneware. Karatsu, Saga Prefecture. Seventeenth century. Height: 14 cm.

69. Road guardian deities (Dōssojin), stone relief rubbing. Nagano Prefecture. Nineteenth century. Height: 68 cm.

70. Mask on temple pillar, wood. Okinawa. ▷
Eighteenth century (prewar photo).

71. Kettle with tripod, iron. Northern Honshu. Seventeenth century. Height: 58 cm.

72. Kettle with lid, iron and wood. Northern Honshu. Seventeenth century.
Height (including lid): 35 cm.

73. Farmer's coat, walnut and Japanese linden. Iwate Prefecture. Height: 134 cm.

74. Costume fragment, stencil-dyed cotton. Aichi Prefecture. Sixteenth century. Height: 43 cm.

75. Six-fold screen by Keisuke Serizawa, stencil-dyed hemp. ▷
Contemporary. Height: 159 cm. (*overleaf*)

76. Teacup, stoneware. Shōji Hamada. Height: 10 cm.

Introduction

This book is a selection from the extensive writings by the late Sōetsu Yanagi, who was the father of the Japanese craft movement, and my close friend for fifty years. I, who am unable to read his original texts, have attempted to translate with the help of able and understanding Japanese assistants, so that readers in the Western world may penetrate that which Buddhism contains for the seeker looking for the meaning of beauty in the face of truth. His chapters are addressed, in the main, to Oriental craftsmen and lovers of craftsmanship, but they are concerned with the very nature of human life and work and are therefore of vital importance to men and women all over the world in our present stage of evolutionary change.

Yanagi was at first a pupil, and later a friend, of the late Dr. Daisetsu Suzuki, whose many books, written by him in English, have made Buddhism known to the West during the last half century. From that background Yanagi has extracted the first aesthetic of Eastern art, which has born fruit in Japan in our time, both in the preservation of the country's folk art and in the recognition and encouragement of artist-craftsmen. Such a man is the potter Shōji Hamada, for example, who continues today the leadership of the strongest national handcraft movement since the Industrial Revolution took place in England.

Emphasis should be laid here upon what Yanagi really did, particularly for Japan and Korea, in discovering the beautiful truthfulness of their domestic handmade crafts. So ordinary as to be unobserved by people at large even though they were the springboard for the Tea masters and their quietism four centuries earlier, folkcrafts were as central to his philosophy as wild flowers to horticulture; this we ourselves perhaps are in danger of forgetting. As he demonstrates with examples again and again in these pages, the purity of the wild flower and the unspoiled countryside so often puts to shame the high culture of town and court. There is a wild and untamable beauty in man when he is in harmony with nature.

This aesthetic is the story of the *seeing eye* of Japan. Let us call it an Eastern perception of significant loveliness. Originally an understanding of the function of true beauty in life, the concept has deteriorated almost from the time of the early Tea masters in the sixteenth century. This was brought about in part by contact with the life and arts of the rest of the world and in part from cultural decay. It was Yanagi's creative thought that began to close this long gap. The publication of this Buddhist aesthetic is the more important because it is a part of that deeper exchange between East and West upon which the pattern of the cultural unification of mankind depends. Many young minds in the West are ripening to feel and eventually understand in their hearts that which moves and inspires Oriental man.

When, following two world wars, the young deny the existence of God, they are confused by what seems to them to be the futility of all religious beliefs in the face of atomic warfare and they protest with disgust at the leaden words of past centuries. They may not know what Yanagi meant when he stood long and silent before the great facade of Chartres; he said, "That is what you have lost. You need a new gospel" Implying any man for everyman, he meant the totality of belief in all mankind. The French built stone upon carved stone visible for thirty miles, lit through coloured glass painted with their dreams and faith— clear-cut as their belief. All men for all men, life for Life Itself. Our disbelief is for lack of wholeness.

I must speak intimately of the Yanagi I knew. His life work was to re-establish art in relationship to the Tree of Life, to God—which is *thusness* to the Buddhist, and from that you cannot escape.

What was Yanagi to me? A question unavoidable and direct. When I was in trouble in Peking in 1917 he came to stay at my Chinese house for a month and persuaded me to go back to Japan, where I lived and worked for a year on his family land at Abiko until one night my workshop burned down. His persuasion was, "Why are you troubled following a mistaken leader? There is no need—the light is in your own work. I have seen it in your pots and drawings. Awake! I have seen it".

> If a man knows not and knows not that he knows not, shun him,
> If a man knows not and knows that he knows not, awaken him,
> If a man knows and knows that he knows, follow him.
> *Arabian saying*

Yanagi lit my lamp.

Yanagi had this also to say about the importance of individual artists. His belief was that with the drying up of the roots of folk art, those with developed intelligence could see that which the simple close-to-earth peasant could not see. He stated that, in consequence, our function at this stage in evolution is that of pilots employing intelligence with humility; thus emerging from isolation and joining hands in the good company of artisans.

Art in Japan is an open sesame. Yanagi sets its criteria at the highest level of total belief. At first reading, some ideas he propounds may appear to contradict our prevalent values, but many people find on reflection that a longer perspective of Western thought reveals counterparts in our own past. His deep reverence for William Blake and Meister Eckhart is an example of what I mean. Differences undoubtedly exist, but extremes touch, and we are the richer thereby if we expand to the full orbit of man's presence on this globe.

I hope and believe that this book will challenge the individual artist and craftsman, because this, our age, is bereft of group, or communal, art; we have lost faith in so much of all but private interpretations of life's meaning. Throughout these pages there is no distinction between truth and beauty, nor basically, between fine and applied art. In Yanagi's "Kingdom of Beauty" all varieties of art—primitive, folk, aristocratic, religious, or individual—meet in equality at a topless, bottomless, round table. This, I think, has never been stated before and may indeed come to be accepted in a mature and round world.

Yanagi was described by Shōji Hamada as a creative critic. Such men are rare, for they help to fashion the character of an epoch. In his case there was a depth of understanding covering the arts and beliefs of the cultures of two hemispheres, penetrating to the roots of all their flowering.

Every artist knows that he is engaged in an encounter with infinity, and that work done with heart and hand is ultimately worship of Life Itself. Sometimes a pot sings out from its wheel-head, from all its related parts, and the potter may pause in himself thinking. "No pattern this time—just a single good glaze—or none at all", and hope that fire will bless with added strength and variety that which his hands have made. Such a pot, or indeed any work of art, is not an expression of the maker alone, but of a degree of enlightenment wherein infinity, however briefly, obliterates the minor self. Herein one may catch a glimpse of Yanagi's width and depth of thought.

The Man and His Work

Sōetsu Yanagi was born in 1889 and died in May, 1961. During the seventy-two years of his life he did many things besides founding the Japanese craft movement and directing its unique museums in Tokyo and elsewhere. He is best known to Western people through the Japan Folkcraft Museum (Mingei-kan) in Tokyo.

It would not be entirely amiss to describe Yanagi's position in Japan as relatively comparable to that of Ruskin and Morris in England. In both cases a deep and comprehensive statement was made regarding work and the qualification of work by beauty, against a background of rapid industrialization. In each case the creative thought behind the resulting movements, separated as they are by approximately one hundred years, may be regarded as counter Industrial Revolutions. Morris and his followers felt that there was no genuine heartbeat left in work and so they set out to print and weave and decorate with their own hands. Seen from the present day they appear almost as romantic and nostalgic as the Pre-Raphaelite painters, but some of their work does not stand up to the reality of the time test. Whether the Japanese will fare better remains to be seen, but this Far Eastern reaction against the overwhelming effects of scientific industrialization at breakneck speed has already lasted forty-two years and has spread all over these islands with more vigour and considerably greater response from the general public than our own movement under Morris generated.

Fundamentally, human beings, whether Eastern or Western, need belief, free play of imagination and intuition in their homes and workshops or they become starved. All the cog-wheels and electronic brains cannot assuage these human needs in the long run. It is for lack of such essentials that we turn to dope of one kind or another, or to destructiveness. Basically this is not so much a revolution against science and the machine as a seeking of a means of counterbalance by employing man's first tools, his own hands, for the expression of his inner nature.

Yanagi was not a craftsman in the sense that Morris was, he did not use his hands, but possessed the extraordinary "seeing eye" of the best masters of Tea, developed in those coteries of fine appreciation—the Tearooms of Japan—on the fringes of monastic life. Neither, in the strict sense, was Yanagi a Tea master. He did not practise the formalities, hinting that no form was preferable to dead form; he was content to await the birth of a new form arising from roots in new life. This is yet to be born of his country, still facing and digesting the thought and life of the West. He, like his friend Hamada, sought rather to assess, to accept, or to reject us at a deeper level.

THE SOCIAL AND POLITICAL POSITION

Japan is not sufficiently familiar to the general English-reading public for fair conclusions to be reached, either about the tasks undertaken by a man like Yanagi or the degree of success attained by him, so I have felt the necessity of attempting to give a broad summary of the general environment of his time as a social and political background to his life and work.

The Meiji Restoration of 1868 and the constitution of some twenty years later marked a sudden leap for the people of Japan from isolated medievalism to the nineteenth century of Queen Victoria. The self-preservatory energies and instincts of a northern Asian people had been called into play by the Black Ships of Commodore Perry demanding the opening of Japan to trade. Astute Japanese minds foresaw and forestalled a fate such as we British imposed on India; it was impossible to fight cannon with swords, so they fought and defeated their Tokugawa shogunate and placed the emperor in power. This provided the law and concentration of energies necessary with which to build up trade, an army and a navy, the money and the security—the primary conditions necessary for the far greater task of understanding and digesting the industrial cultures of the West.

Year by year the best young brains were sent abroad to learn: to England for naval and financial tutelage, to Germany for scientific and military knowledge, and to France for art. I think it may be said without fear of contradiction that no nation, certainly no Oriental nation, has faced so vast a task with comparable determination and energy. I have often wondered whether Britain of the fifteenth century, an offshore kingdom with an historical position curiously similar to Japan's, could have done as well in like circumstances. Self-protective wars were involved, first with China, and subsequently Russia, but the expenditure of money and life was nothing in comparison to that of energy spent absorbing the thought behind the civilizations of Western man.

What was the hidden source of this energy? I am inclined to ascribe it to the inherent power of the native religion of Japan—Shinto. J. W. T. Mason in his book, *The Meaning of Shinto* says, "The creative activities of the Japanese, individualized and co-ordinated afresh, moved forth from mediaevalism into the modern world, showing the same eager desires as in the past for new knowledge and accomplishments, while retaining many aspects of the ancient ways of the race". This ancient and subconscious urge of creative life was canalized and used deliberately, I believe, by leaders of the military party after the ending of the Anglo-Japanese alliance, and eventually built up into the formidable theory of race supremacy that led to Pearl Harbor and Japan's ultimate defeat in the last war. Initial success went to Japan's head as it went to Hitler's. But it should not be forgotten that an economic cause was at work as well—the fearful overcrowding of these islands, which still remains an unsolved problem. When I came to Japan in 1909 the population was fifty million and now it is a hundred and five million, living off less arable land than the British Isles contain. Another factor, little appreciated both in Japan as well as abroad, is the profound inferiority complex engendered by the fact that Japan entered the family of nations so late and so poor. Psychologically it is not surprising that a people thus handicapped should, under stress, in a secondary stage of inferiority, become bombast and aggressive.

Neither is it just that the Japanese should be so lightly accused of mere imitation. They are facile and quick to see and act, being descendants, not only of the Mongol, but also of the Malay. During the long centuries since the first waves of Buddhism broke upon these shores in the seventh century, the people assimilated the cultures of the mainland, just as we did in England. Now they are set, first, to understand all that we have to offer, and, eventually, to digest what they have learned and to produce new mutations. Some results are already taking us by surprise and leading the world in science, industry, and art. This cannot be done by mere adroit imitation. What we have called Japanese imitativeness is a first and unavoidable stage of understanding the unfamiliar. It involves many errors before truth is found.

As I have already indicated, Japan was emerging from a long hibernation of interned medieval life when I first met a young Yanagi fresh from the Peer's School and the Imperial University, in 1910. His father was of high rank in the navy, and several of his friends belonged to the nobility surrounding the emperor in the old Kyoto court. They were a brilliant group, some of whom became well-known writers. In that same year they started a monthly magazine, the *Shirakaba* ("Silver Birch"), which in the following thirteen years led progressive thought in the study of Western literature, art, and philosophy. Yanagi, as one of its editors, was chiefly interested in artists and mystics. With an enthusiasm that I shared, these young men searched the horizons of Western art and thought, ancient and modern. Progressively educated, but traditionally Oriental, they selected and reappraised our artists and authors from, let us say, Giotto as an artist and Meister Eckhart as a mystic, through the High Renaissance, into all our movements in art and literature up to the present day. I remember, vividly, a long night in Yanagi's room when we unpacked a dozen large German colour reproductions of paintings by Cezanne and Van Gogh. They shook us into immediate recognition, and, when republished, the responses of all literary as well as artistic circles in the land were touched. Yanagi said to me of Cezanne, "He is a doorway between East and West," and of Rembrandt, "He is one of our artists." I introduced him to William Blake, as poet, artist, and mystic. Yanagi bit hard on that bait. Colour plates arrived from England, and he toured provincial towns to show and talk about them. The response was immediate, and in that one tour more of those expensive and numbered prints were sold than in Blake's *Albion* to date. Then in 1914 he wrote a thick volume on William Blake, and the lothful publisher was astounded at its success. Blake's *Fourfold Vision* was no mystery to this Oriental, and he was able to convince his countrymen of its validity. From Blake, Yanagi went to Walt Whitman, whom he regarded as the great American poet. Later on, between 1929 and 1930 after a year as lecturer on Buddhist art and aesthetics at Harvard, he published a little magazine in Japan called *Blake and Whitman*.

In 1918 Yanagi persuaded me to return from Peking, where I had spent a couple of First World War years, and build a kiln and workshop on his family property at Abiko, some twenty-five miles east of Tokyo. He had already begun to take much interest in Korean crafts, particularly pottery. Living beside a kiln deepened this attraction and caused him to consider the issues of craftsmanship in our time, especially the transitions attendant upon the change from local folkcrafts to individual, or artist craftsmanship. Naturally the English movement under William Morris was the subject of much discussion, and I clearly recollect how he questioned me about an equivalent term for peasant or folk art, in Japanese. No word existed, and he finally composed the word *mingei*, which means "art of the people" and has now become part of the Japanese language. Towards the end of a year of rich exchange of ideas between Yanagi and his friends of the *Shirakaba* magazine, myself, and others who came to visit the little colony at Abiko, a young man called Hamada appeared, who told me that he had decided to become a potter after training at the Tokyo Institute of Technology. He was the first man I had ever met who could talk to me about the chemistry and geology of clay and glaze, for my master, the sixth Kenzan, only knew how things were done in a limited field and could not explain why. We liked each other at first sight, and eventually Hamada asked if I would take him to England with me when I returned home in a year's time. When my workshop burned down, a kiln was built for me in Tokyo, and during the last year Hamada visited me again. It was finally agreed that he would travel with me and my family, and he helped start my pottery at St. Ives, where he stayed for three years. He returned to Japan in 1923, finally settling at Mashiko, whence he came to know Yanagi well. In 1926 he and Yanagi and Hamada's old potter friend Kanjirō Kawai visited the mountain monasteries of Kōya-san and there determined to start a Japanese Craft Society —the Mingei-kai.

The decision to start a craft society was momentous, for it shaped the lives of those most concerned from that time forward. It led not only to the growth of a stronger movement than in England, but also to a return wave of cultural influence strengthened by a new content from the Far West.

The next step was the publication of a craft magazine, *Kōgei* ("Crafts"). Between 1931 and 1941, 120 issues were published, and there has been no other publication on its level. The covers—no two the same—by paper makers, textile artists, and lacquerers; the illustrations, the intimate articles by craftsmen; actual samples of papers and textiles still being made; the high selectivity; the awakening of Japan to her own living treasures; the far-seeing leadership—again Yanagi was the editor.

By 1936 private support had grown to such an extent that the present Japan Folkcraft Museum was built in Tokyo. It houses many thousand examples of Japanese and Korean crafts, old and new, and of other countries as well, beautifully displayed and constantly changed. It is the focal point of the movement, but at Kurashiki, in Okayama Prefecture, there is another unique craft museum housed in architecturally fine old fireproof storehouses, and there are smaller museums in Tottori, Osaka, and other cities as well. But the work is not only carried out in museums —the objects furnish restaurants and hotels and are sold in craft shops all over Japan.

The Future of Crafts

The facts have to be faced concerning the future of craftsmanship any-where within an industrial civilization and about what Yanagi has to say about this in the following chapters. Before the age of science and modern industry, crafts used to spring out of the hearts and hands of man.

Not long ago questions were thrust at Hamada and myself by a keen young journalist from one of the leading dailies on behalf of a younger generation who eyed with suspicion the word *mingei*. Hamada handled him with so much understanding and wisdom that after a couple of hours he fell silent and quietly offered his thanks. This was the best and deepest discussion on the road forward for craftsmen that I have heard. Hamada said in effect that we were as sick of the word *mingei* as we were of the opposed word *sakka*, meaning the current so-called individual or artist-craftsman. He said they had become, equally, misconceptions of Yanagi's intentions. Someone tried to quell the young journalist, but he would not be shaken off and, turning to me, asked what I considered craft to be. "Good work proceeding from the whole man, heart, head, and hand, in proper balance", I replied. Then he went on, "How do we obtain that in our society now?" Hamada broke in at this point saying that he had met one man in America, Charles Eames, who had shown a way forward. He described the first meeting, together with Yanagi and myself, at his home near Los Angeles in 1954. He laid stress upon Eames's open acceptance both of the contemporary scientific and industrial world as well as the traditions of the past; upon his playful refusal to be chained by fear, and his constant inventiveness and domination of the mechanical by a new freedom of intuition and joy in making. He was saying, in fact, that the inner had regained control of the outer in this man, which I think goes to the root of the matter.

At this point in time we are trying to face the problem of how to make best use of the individual craftsman, who is displacing the traditional craftsman. Regarding this issue it was Yanagi, Hamada, and myself who had found in Denmark the use of a new kind of designer of furniture for contemporary life. There a bridge was thrown across the chasm that has long kept handcraftsmen and designers in industry apart. Danish architects started with practise before theory. They only came to their drawing boards after an apprenticeship in handling wood, stone, brick, etc. Therefore they embraced and understood both the hand and the machine and could and did employ both. Some of this work, made entirely by hand, was expensive, other examples, made partly with the use of machinery, was moderately priced, but the greatest number were cheap and were made entirely by mechanical means.

If I am right in my belief that "theory before practise" has been at the root of a division that has kept the two camps at daggers drawn ever since the Industrial Revolution took place—particularly in England where it started—then we owe the Danes gratitude for having found a canker at the root and for providing a new source of industrial designers in the future whose vision is sufficiently expanded. The mistake was, I believe, in putting theory before practise, and this affected not only work, but also our concept of education. This does not imply a necessity for all craftsmen to become designers for industry, but it does indicate a liberation from a nineteenth century bondage of the spirit, a prison of rationalism, materialism, and individualism.

I have left the last question concerning individual craftsmanship to the end. The problem is how artist-craftsmen are to function rightly in a world of machines. Probing further, one is forced to ask what the function of an artist-craftsman is and why has Yanagi given him his full support? The appearance of one hundred thousand potters alone, outside industry, in the United States after the last war indicates that the gap was not being filled. Clearly something was lacking that mechanized labour did not supply. I have often called it the heartbeat in work. Enthusiasm and play of imagination, for example, occur as wet clay spins under fingers, but take place with varying degrees of intensity, depending on how free of inhibitions one is. Both the creative gift and the freedom are essential. In an artist-craftsman it is the degree of life force canalized into a craft. The degree; the purity; the intensity. We can relate the work of individuals to the magnificent communal creations of unknown, humble and usually illiterate artisans of past ages and draw inspiration from them.

It is this kind of work to which Sōetsu Yanagi persistently referred. His main criticism of individual craftsmen and modern artists is that they are overproud of their individualism. I think I am right in saying Yanagi's belief was that the good artist or craftsman has no personal pride because in his soul he knows that any prowess he shows is evidence of that Other Power. Therefore what Yanagi says is "Take heed of the humble; be what you are by birthright; there is no room for arrogance".

Handcraftsmanship, if it be alive, justifies itself at any time as an intimate expression of the spirit of man. Such work is an end in itself and not a means to an end. If, however, it ceases to serve a functional need, it runs the risk of becoming art for art's sake and untrue to its nature, depending upon the sincerity of the craftsman. Who is in a better position to teach the young co-ordination of their human faculties? Who should know so well the experimental side of design on material? That we need a new kind of designer has been demonstrated by the Danish architects; that creative design for mechanical reproduction requires fresh, free, leadership is shown by Eames and his like.

One other thing seems necessary—the *seeing eye*. Without it, selectivity lacks standard. Here, in the relationship of truth to beauty, maybe, Japan makes its greatest contribution to world culture.

YANAGI'S LOVE OF KOREA

My friend had a great sympathy for Korea, its people and its arts. Especially, he loved the pots of the Yi dynasty. I recall one day in 1918 at Abiko, just after he had returned from a visit to Seoul. When, at the hour for lunch, I joined him in his study overlooking the lagoon of Teganuma, I found him in a reverie, slowly moving from pot to pot, gently stroking each in turn. After a pause I asked him what he was doing. He turned and said quietly, "I am visiting my Korean friends". Though the same pots are now in the museum, he is not . . . or is he?

The Japanese people find a unique language of aesthetic communication in pottery, and, as Yanagi said, "Japan is a potter's Paradise".

It was his enthusiasm for Yi porcelains more than anything else that popularized them, and, incidentally, caused their prices to soar—now they are fabulous. In fact the prices of pots both old and new are higher in Japan than anywhere else.

Yanagi went to Korea many times. I went with him twice, and we climbed the Diamond Mountains together in 1935 before I took the Trans-Siberian back to Paris.

After the occupation of Korea, the heavy hand of Japanese militarism fell upon The Land of Morning Calm. It became unsafe to raise a voice in protest, but Yanagi, an anti-militarist, went to Seoul and started a small museum in one of the old palace buildings, where Japanese and Koreans could meet in the common enjoyment of Korean art, leaving politics aside and thereby avoiding possible offence to the government.

Before ending this section concerning Yanagi and Korea, it is worth reminding the reader that the Japanese Tea ceremony was built round Korean rice bowls and that contemporary Japanese potters such as Kenkichi Tomimoto, Kanjirō Kawai, and Hamada were deeply influenced by Yi porcelain.

In Conclusion

Whilst translating these thoughts of Yanagi's line by line and word by word, as an artist-craftsman I have had a sense of doubt on one main issue—the relationship between the conscious artist and the comparatively unconscious craftsman. Yanagi's constantly reiterated theme concerns the exceeding difficulties experienced in attaining a like purity and wholeness by the artist. He says our arts and crafts are in a diseased condition—with that I agree—but he turns to the artist-craftsman to act as the pilot in this dilemma because of his greater awareness, thereby indicating the power that has come to conscious man through the evolution of intellect. The results are not the same—Bach is not plainsong, Michaelangelo is not Mokujiki (Plate 41), and Hamada's bowls are not Ō Ido (Plate 1). But they are as flowers, cultivated or wild, and who is to say which are more beautiful at that round table of Heaven? . . . I have so wished that I could ask him questions once again, or argue with him on some of the issues that he raises. My own view is that we have reached a stage when individual intellectualism has become necessary for survival, but that we were caught in a net of means towards ends of which we have almost lost sight, and this net has been cast all over the world. Yanagi is the first critic to restate those ends out of the Buddhist basis of human aspiration.

I have felt obliged to preserve his style, which at times is repetitive like a carpenter's hammer; but a house had to be built, and Japanese carpenters are perfectionists.

In all our years of friendship, and in living with Yanagi, I can recall no harsh word between us, but it was inevitable that he made enemies. He was devoted all his life through to unswerving purposes. One of them was the establishment of a unique home for the treasures of beauty produced by the unknown craftsman, which his incredibly sharp eyes found where nobody else had looked before. It is not an exaggeration to say that he discovered both Korean and Japanese folk art. In his indefatigable search for the foundations upon which to build his temple of beauty inevitably he trod on some toes, and at times he may have appeared severe. He gathered together his unique collection with one-pointed intensity, almost avidly. To some people it may have seemed that this was for himself; indeed, in one sense it was, because through his own joy and satisfaction those eyes of his developed the vision and perception that enabled him to leave a museum of crafts as a permanent national collection of such unrivalled loveliness. He also left as a legacy to all men an aesthetic and religious creed of far more than national import, of which the following pages are a part.

Wherever I have travelled in Japan I found his memory venerated. At his funeral service in his folkcraft museum, attended by over one thousand people, the great Buddhist scholar, Dr. Daisetsu Suzuki, then aged ninety, broke down as he spoke of his friend and pupil, and out of the quiet of shared emotion whispered, "That the old should die is natural, but that the young should go before their time. . . ".

Japanese seldom show their feelings in public, but I was told that Shōji Hamada was the only speaker whose voice remained steady. Under his ungrudged leadership Yanagi's great work goes on.

Many times since Yanagi died, as I have struggled with the hard edges of his written thought, there has been a keen awareness of his living presence. He still speaks silently in his quiet room at the back of the folkcraft museum, where nothing has been moved: his chair, flowers in a Korean vase, his books, his photograph hanging on the wall. . . .

Bernard Leach

Towards a Standard of Beauty

THE JAPAN FOLKCRAFT MUSEUM

I CANNOT FORGET THE NIGHT in January, 1926, when, in company with Kanjirō Kawai and Shōji Hamada at the great mountain monastery of Kōya-san, we made the decision to start a national collection of folk arts. It was a great night preceded by years of preparatory thought. The love of things of beauty had been mine since school days. I had collected small pieces of old Imari porcelain, particularly saké bottles, from childhood, but it was while travelling in Korea that this interest burst into flame, fifty-four years ago. I have been to Korea at various times, and my love and respect for its crafts has continued to grow. I always returned loaded with trophies. In those early days, pots of the Koryo dynasty (936–1392) were expensive, and I could not afford them, but work of the later Yi dynasty (1392–1910) was quite cheap. The beauty of these pieces attracted me much more, so I arranged a small exhibition of objects of the Yi dynasty in Tokyo in 1921. However, at that period my feeling was that the Korean people needed a folk museum badly, and so I contrived to get a small building in the old palace in Seoul devoted to that purpose and filled it with Korean pots and other crafts. Most of them were of the Yi period. It was still there at the time of World War II, but what happened to the articles during the Korean War I do not know. Having accomplished that work, my thought turned to my own country and its similar need of discovery and collection of things of truth and beauty for the sake of the future. So I began to gather Japanese crafts. By the late 1920s I already had a large number and was feeling the lack of space in

UNIVERSITY COLLEGE
101
LIBRARY
SWANSEA

my house. The time was ripe, and it was at this point that the meeting described above took place.

We had many dreams, and slowly realized how much money any one of them would cost. I approached the authorities in the Tokyo National Museum, suggesting that some space should be allotted to my idea of crafts, in which case we would contribute what we collected. The museum at this time had almost no folkcrafts worthy of the name, and we thought they would accept them gladly; but whether they attached no value to the objects as such or simply had not the space, there was no reply at all. This was to prove a blessing, for it meant that we were to have our own independent museum that would become known all over the world. However, the founding of the museum was to require another five years.

In 1929 I made a journey to Europe with Mr. Hamada and visited the Skansen Folk Museum in Stockholm. We came away more determined than ever, and also with the feeling that we could exercise more discretion and make a display of good things only.

In 1935, with the help of many friends, the advice of the late Tamesaburō Yamamoto and the substantial contributions of the late Magosaburō Ohara, the building was begun. My long-cherished dream was coming true, with what joy to me I cannot describe.

A house originally intended for my own personal use was made into one wing of the museum. It was an old, long gatehouse, built partly of stone, and brought in piecemeal from Hamada's countryside. The main museum building was built to harmonize with it, to the derision of many moderns. We did not employ foreign architecture. A quiet white light penetrated into the interior through Japanese paper windows. By arrangement with the government, the contents of the museum were free of taxation in return for making them a gift to the nation in perpetuity. I have learned a lesson from seeing many wonderful private collections of art that were due for dispersal at the close of their owner's lives. At the time when I attained the age of sixty-one, which in Japan is specially celebrated, I received so many fine craft gifts from my friends and from those whom I had helped that I decided to make all my property and possessions concerned with crafts, including a library of books, a part of the Japan Folkcraft Museum. This I did with a sense of relief, in much the same way as with a religious gift. The name, Japan Folkcraft Museum (Nihon Mingei-kan), is not mere words: it stands for the arts of the people, returned to the people.

The war brought two threats to the museum. First a great fire caused by incendiary bombs burned to within a few feet of the building, when the wind veered. Later came the decision by the American forces to commandeer my house, which was only countermanded by the representations of an American friend of Japanese crafts, who was head of the Red Cross, Beth Blake.

The bulk of the contents of the museum are representative examples of the country crafts of the Japanese people. It is my belief that while the high level of culture of any country can be found in its fine arts, it is also vital that we should be able to examine and enjoy the proofs of the culture of the great mass of the people, which we call folk art. The former are made by a few for a few, but the latter, made by the many for many, are a truer test. The quality of the life of the people of that country as a whole can best be judged by the folkcrafts. The main objective of the folkcraft museum is to allow this to be done. A visit will convince any open mind of the great beauty that the simple and ordinary men and women of the countrysides of Japan put into the work of their hands, despite a long history of war, earthquake, and fire. There was little freedom in old Japanese society, the hand of the samurai was very oppressive, but out of the life of the mass of the people these fresh flowers bloomed. The life of people themselves unfortunately is not given much attention by historians: one reads about the aristocracy and the great. I hope this museum will be a slight corrective.

Sometimes, in the past, instead of heavy monetary taxes governments enacted tax in kind, as, for example, in the case of the lovely textiles of the Ryūkyū Islands, and yet those gay and harmonious fabrics continued to blossom forth. One wonders why. How does one explain the fact that after the Meiji Restoration in 1868 and the uplifting of this burden on the poor, such a change for the worse in the quality of their products took place? I think the answer is to be found in the spread of wholesale trading. The profit-making motive became uppermost, and the change from the age of the hand to the age of the machine took place; the two together have had a disastrous effect not only on the crafts but also on the way of natural life in which they had their roots. The new industrialized life is freer. Why, then, did the crafts flourish under social oppression? Apparently, despite its weight, the people were really more at liberty to live their country life supported by their Buddhist beliefs, and even by their superstitions. They accepted the picture of life as it was given to them, with its balance of good and evil under heaven, without question or protest. That made the struggle bearable and even left room for the play of the life spirit in their rice fields and the work of their hands, their crafts.

Religion is derided by Communism as an appendix of slavish ignorance, but what has Communism got to offer the hungry spirit? I have studied and thought about the flowering of the crafts of mankind for a long time and always find that I come back to the mothering care of the beliefs of man. What a great debt we owe them.

Looking back over two thousand years of Japanese history, in the early period, up to the ninth century, national life was centred in the power, both secular and religious, of the emperor. Then power passed to the Fujiwara family and the aristocracy. Meanwhile, the gentle pacifying and spiritualizing effect of Buddhism was spreading through the land, so that in the following Kamakura era (1185–1333) the determining factors of social life were the sword on one side and the rosary on the other. After that came the Ashikaga era (1333–1573), in which the religion, having permeated the whole country, was flowering in all the arts and crafts. Finally we arrive at the long Tokugawa shogunate (1603–1868), which gave Japan over 250 years of peaceful isolation in which to digest foreign influences and to produce those crafts of which this museum is full.

Since the Meiji Restoration, the overwhelming influx of Western ideas has had such an effect that today the mass of the people neither know nor wish to know their inheritance as Japanese. They regard everything from the West as new and progressive and everything traditional as retrogressive. Emulation is one thing, and this blind imitation in the belief that something new is being achieved is misguided because the only true, and at the same time new, things can grow from Japanese roots. Truth is both old and new.

I would like to believe that beauty is of deep import to our modern age. Without question, the intention of morality, philosophy, and religious belief is to bring hope, joy, peace, and freedom to mankind. But in our time religion has lost its grip. Intellectualism has undermined spiritual aspiration in most people. At this juncture I would put the question, might not beauty, and the love of the beautiful, perhaps bring peace and harmony? Could it not carry us forward to new concepts of life's meaning? Would it not establish a fresh concept of culture? Would it not be a dove of peace between the various cultures of mankind?

THE INDIVIDUAL CRAFTSMAN AND THE FOLK CRAFTSMAN

The ordinary idea regarding fine arts is simply to exhibit them to be seen, but the folkcraft museum aims to provide standards for beauty and even a meeting place where one may come into contact with the religion of beauty. I would like the visitor not so much to "meet the craftsman at home" as to see how such things fit into everyday life and to take home some ideas for enriching his own life. The other aim is to provide hints as to what should be produced in the future. The first aim has relevance for the user, the second to the maker and seller.

I feel that the great problem is how to make good things in the present state of society. I wish that everyone would realize that until recently beauty in things was commonplace and that it is our responsibility to demand that of the future. From the things exhibited here I would like to pass on the power to do so.

This is not a place where things are actually made, but there are many craftsmen in our ranks and among our leaders. We hold exhibitions, moreover, of new work both of traditional and of individual crafts. The importance of the latter lies not only in their individual merit but also in their pathfinding significance.

I am asked from time to time if the individualism of such work is not in opposition to the character of traditional crafts. Certainly the nature of individual work is different, but the closeness of the relationship between the two is very important for the future. The individual craftsmen whose work is shown at the museum are all lovers and respecters of folkcraft, and they are very good friends. There are other individual artists who dismiss as unimportant traditional crafts and craftsmen. I wonder why their own work is so poor.

If they had the eyes to see with and the will to ponder over what they saw, instead of exhibiting arrogance or mere learning, the situation would be different. There is so much to learn and to respect—the true individual, or artist, craftsman does so, that is why he is a friend. Those who do not do so have no capacity for self-examination, and that is why their work is poor. The individual craftsman of today has the potentiality of shepherding craftsmanship towards a rebirth of true work. Work without innate beauty is dead work; that is why the artist-craftsman is important to us. The great need of our time is for the artist-craftsman not only to produce his own good work but also to ally himself closely with the artisan, so that eventually we may have beauty in common things again.

This kind of artist or craftsman is a part of society. He only qualifies his name when he joins forces with the designer. Through his efforts alone can the leadership either in the countryside or in the factory be established. For lack of this guiding hand, crafts are dying everywhere, and industry itself does not know which way to turn in matters of design and continues to produce what we have unfortunately grown accustomed to.

The country craftsman does not know how to deal with the changes of fashion and their demands in the cities. Exporters and importers of industrial goods have little thought beyond profit and loss. In both cases the discriminating eye, which is the faculty of the artist, is not being called into use. This is the position as I see it.

HANDWORK AND MACHINE WORK

Almost all the things in the folkcraft museum are handmade. The period of handmade goods was extremely long, and during the mere fifty or sixty years of Japanese industrialism it can hardly be expected that the objects produced are very good or beautiful. Even during these years, however, handwork has continued alongside the machine; the folkcraft museum collection naturally contains examples of this recent work.

Members of the younger generation frequently tell me that the age of handwork is passed, that the increase in population has made machine production a necessity in order to produce enough at a low enough price. There is also no doubt that the modern sensibility is more attracted by machine-made beauty, and that young people tend to look on a taste for handcrafts as out of date. I understand this; I have had it brought up so many times that it has become stale, but the issue is not so simple as this. Such is the age of the machine, and many think that science can achieve anything and that religion is banished together with hand labour. But there are others who think that religion is all the more needed at such a time. It must be recognized that the machine has in its nature more power than the hand and that there is a limit to what the hand can do, but just as the hand has its limitations, so does the machine.

106

As we all know, America is the home of the machine; there has never been much handwork there since the beginning of its modern history. Most articles are made by machine—yet, ever since the last war, it is there that a new move towards handwork has taken place. Even the universities are teaching handcrafts as part of their curricula, especially pottery and weaving. Why has this strange thing happened? England started the Industrial Revolution, and the beauty of products deteriorated. In protest, William Morris's arts and crafts movement arose and spread all over Europe. Again why did this happen? The answer is that so many shoddy and badly designed goods caused protest. Moreover, the nature of machine work is such that its products are standardized and thus monotonous and cold, ill-fitted to serve as man's companions in his daily life. Human nature is complex and in the long run cannot put up with this. The situation is considerably worsened by the combination of machine production with the modern large-scale profit motive of commerce. These together have the effect of spoiling the quality of raw materials and of lessening the hours of labour for the sake of greater gain. Satisfaction in work itself decreases. Because the workers have no outlet of expression, the products are heartless. To remedy all this, first of all good designers are needed. But there are hardly any. Even if there were many, designers would require complete support from management. At present, for lack of both good designers and industrial support, the good article is a rarity. That is why there have been these reactions in both England and America.

On reflection, one must conclude that in bringing cheap and useful goods to the average household, industrialism has been of service to mankind—but at the cost of the heart, of warmth, friendliness, and beauty. By contrast, articles well made by hand, though expensive, can be enjoyed in homes for generations, and, this considered, they are not expensive after all. Is spendthrift replacement economical? Rapid turnover of goods is the salesman's policy, especially in America. It seems to me that there is something so basic, so natural in the hand that the urge to utilize its power will always make itself felt. Moreover, the chief characteristic of handcrafts is that they maintain by their very nature a direct link with the human heart, so that the work always partakes of a human quality. Machine-made things are children of the brain; they are not very human. The more they spread, the less the human being is needed. What seems to be a great advance is also a great step backward;

the desire for the natural as opposed to the artificial surely has some basic, unchanging significance.

No machine can compare with a man's hands. Machinery gives speed, power, complete uniformity, and precision, but it cannot give creativity, adaptability, freedom, heterogeneity. These the machine is incapable of, hence the superiority of the hand, which no amount of rationalism can negate. Man prefers the creative and the free to the fixed and standardized.

The machine, of course, came into being for man's use and advantage; therefore, we need not avoid it but should find a way of using it more cleverly than we have done hitherto. The problem is not a matter of either hand or machine, but of utilizing both. We have yet to discover just what is suitable work for each. To this end, again, it is a truly new kind of designer that is needed. He must, in the first place, know beauty at sight; then it is essential that he should understand the principles of mechanics and their operation in industry yet at the same time must also appreciate fully the value of handwork. Such designers could make machine-made products better and healthier. But they must not forget that the machine, too, has its limitations. The best course, probably, is that handwork and the machine should co-operate and supplement each other's shortcomings. This had already happened in the industrial arts in Denmark.

Beyond all question of old or new, the human hand is the ever-present tool of human feeling, whereas the machine, however new, is soon out of date. Young people nowadays judge according to whether a thing is new or old, but more important is whether it is true or false. If true, whether it is handmade or machine-made, it will always preserve its newness.

Finally, to protect the financial interests of the makers, whether using the hand or machine, from the octopus of wholesaling, they should form associations or guilds in the interest of honest craftsmanship. To this end, an advance in the ethics of production is essential, as is a deepening of the religious sense in everyday life. The question of handcrafts is not simply technological or economic, but, basically, a spiritual question. Both handwork and machine work will go astray if there is not spiritual preparation. In this sense, the many objects in the Japan Folkcraft Museum should provide an endless source of inspiration for the crafts—the handmade objects of the future—for they show, always, what is true work.

1954

Seeing and Knowing

SEEING AND KNOWING are often separate. Nothing could be more admirable than when they coincide, but only too often they remain estranged. In some fields this does not matter, but in the areas of aesthetics or art history or the like, any gap between perception and knowledge assumes fatal proportions. This is an obvious fact that is too frequently overlooked. Similar cases are common in other fields as well.

The critic of religion, for example, who has no religious feelings has no force in his criticisms. In the same way, the moralist who does not live by his theories carries no weight, however brilliant he may be. I know many famous art critics who have no feeling of beauty, and I cannot therefore respect their knowledge. They may be learned, but it avails nothing. It is the same with philosophy and history. The student of philosophy and the philosopher should be distinguished; a man who knows a great deal about history is not necessarily a historian.

Doubtless many would reply that intuitive perception of beauty is incomplete without learning, that without knowledge one does not see a thing as a whole. Socrates saw the identity of action and knowing. To see and at the same time to comprehend is the ideal, but in practise we are far removed from this unity. The things to be seen and the knowledge to be gained have so vastly increased in this modern age that man's activities have been pushed either into one direction or the other. But of the two, those forced into the field of knowledge are in the worse position as far as beauty is concerned.

To be unable to *see* beauty properly is to lack the basic foundation for any aesthetic understanding. One should refrain from becoming a student of aesthetics just because one has a good brain; to know a lot about beauty is no qualification. Seeing and knowing form an exterior and an interior, not a right and a left. Either way, they are not equal. In understanding beauty, intuition is more of the essence than intellectual perception.

The reversal of these two faculties stultifies vision. To "see" is to go direct to the core; to know the facts about an object of beauty is to go around the periphery. Intellectual discrimination is less essential to an understanding of beauty than the power of intuition that precedes it.

Beauty is a kind of mystery, which is why it cannot be grasped adequately through the intellect. The part of it available to intellection lacks depth. This might seem to be a denial of aesthetics, but it is as Aquinas said: "No one shows such a knowledge of God as he who says that one can know nothing". Aquinas was one of the greatest minds of medieval times and knew well how foolish his own wisdom was in the face of God. No one could rival the wisdom with which he acknowledged the poverty of his own mind. Though he is renowned as a theologian, he was surely still greater as a man of faith; without that fact he would have been a commonplace intellectual.

He who only knows, without seeing, does not understand the mystery. Even should every detail of beauty be accounted for by the intellect, does such a tabulation lead to beauty? Is the beauty that can be neatly reckoned really profound? The scholar of aesthetics tends to base his ideas on knowledge—or rather, he tries to make seeing proceed from knowing. But this is a reversal of the natural order of things.

The eye of knowledge cannot, thereby, see beauty. What is the beauty that a man of erudition sees as he holds a fine pot in his hands? If he picks a wild flower to pieces, petal by petal, and counts them, and tries to put them together again, can he regain the beauty that was there? All the assembly of dead parts cannot bring life back again. It is the same with knowing. One cannot replace the function of seeing by the function of knowing. One may be able to turn intuition into knowledge, but one cannot produce intuition out of knowledge. Thus the basis of aesthetics must not be intellectual concepts. For this purpose all the classification in the world avails nothing, and the scholar does not even become a good student of aesthetics. There are so many whose voices invariably rise round works of art, trying to pin them down in neat categories, always preceding the verification of beauty with such questions as "who made it, when, and where". The recognition of date and school, etc. is a matter of pride for them. They are intensely ashamed of leaving any mystery unaccounted for in their explanations. This is commonly referred to as the "academic conscience". In fact, I suspect it is because they have not better work to do, or cannot do it properly.

The man in the street is hoodwinked, he thinks he is being informed by a man who really does know everything. Should we apply the adjective "good" to such critics and art historians? How their writings on art are flooded with exaggerated and strained expressions. They use words, too, in remarkable numbers. They cannot suggest beauty without great heaps of adjectives.

When the power to see does not accompany the power to know—when the power to see is blunted—art historians, critics, and collectors all fall into the same kind of confusion. Even assuming that they correctly praise beautiful things, they will also, without fail, praise the ugly as well. This shows that, ultimately, they are not even praising the beautiful for the right reasons. Their blurred eyesight is incapable of distinguishing beauty and ugliness. They have not grasped the yardstick of beauty. They study things that have no place in history and cheerfully rank the good and bad side by side. They have no sense of values, when they are right, they are right by luck. Beauty is essentially a matter of values; if values are confused, if there are no standards, if valueless things are admitted among the valued, judgements of beauty lose their basis.

The number of collectors of art in the world is constantly increasing, but there are few whose perceptions are developed enough to gather various types of art together with a uniformity of standard and taste. This is undoubtedly due to the foot-rule approach that I am decrying. As great an importance is placed on secondary issues, for example the idea that because something is expensive it is necessarily good. It may be rare, or unblemished, or be inscribed with the name of a famous artist, but these are all tradesman's arguments or tactics, after all, and have nothing to do with beauty. These good people are deceived in this way because they have not got eyes to see with. If they had, they would not be concerned with rarity, perfect condition, or former ownership. There is no real point in collecting unless for the sake of beauty, nor is it truly possible for those who cannot see, for if they persist, their collections are bound to be a jumble of good and bad. This is the inevitable result of putting a foot-rule between ones eyes and an object.

To look at the question from a different angle, seeing relates to the concrete, knowing to the abstract. Let us say that we have a painting by Tawaraya Sōtatsu in front of us: it is an object that the eyes see and research, and to which one's heart can respond, but the knower with the foot-rule is immediately busy with a dozen questions as to age, authenticity, previous ownership, technique and the like. These secondary and circumferential matters are all very well only if they lead to a better appreciation of Sōtatsu's painting. Without such appreciation all the knowledge in the world will take one nowhere. Thereby it becomes clear that both to see and to know is best, but that in any case seeing comes first. See first and know afterwards.

Seeing is a born faculty, knowledge is acquired. To a point anyone can acquire knowledge, but the potential of seeing is born with us. Although some are more gifted than others, it is generally accepted that the musical or the artistic gifts are born with us and that there is nothing to be done about it if one is not so fortunate. The gift of seeing is of the same order. This leaves the ungifted forlorn. I would like to give them three pieces of advice.

First, put aside the desire to judge immediately; acquire the habit of just looking. Second, do not treat the object as an object for the intellect. Third, just be ready to receive, passively, without interposing yourself. If you can void your mind of all intellectualization, like a clear mirror that simply reflects, all the better. This nonconceptualization—the Zen state of *mushin* ("no mind")—may seem to represent a negative attitude, but from it springs the true ability to contact things directly and positively.

1940

Pattern

Some years ago I attempted to write on this very difficult subject, but gave up in dissatisfaction with my own grasp of the matter. Yet whenever I consider the question of beauty, I return to this subject, so close, I feel, is the relationship between transformation into beauty and transformation into pattern. To divine the significance of pattern is the same as to understand beauty itself. So, at least, it seems to me. The relationship between beauty in the crafts and pattern is particularly profound.

As a concrete example, take the five-leaf bamboo grass crest motif (Plate 23) used on our Japanese clothes. To most of us it is so commonplace as not to be given any thought, but I think it is an excellent example of what I mean. What sort of pattern is this? Why is it beautiful? What are the conditions for a "good pattern"?

Comparing this pattern and the plant, the pattern immediately suggests bamboo grass, but even a first glance shows that it is not a literal representation. A pattern is both true to nature and artificial.

Where lies the essential difference between the plant and the pattern? The plant is a product of nature. The pattern is this plus a human viewpoint. The original plant is still "raw", nothing more than the given material. The viewpoint is what gives it content. Without a viewpoint, seeing is no different from not seeing. Everybody can *see* the plant; but not everybody sees it in the same way, much less perceives its beauty. Beauty only emerges in the plant with the addition of a viewpoint that sees it as beautiful. Bamboo grass pattern is, in a sense, bamboo grass provided with order by a viewpoint. All patterns are products of a viewpoint. For that reason, patterns are not reproductions of nature, but new creations. What is this viewpoint? What should man look at? In what way ought he to look?

There are many ways of seeing, but the truest and best is with the intuition, for it takes in the whole, whereas the intellect only takes in a part. Pattern is born when one reproduces the intuitively perceived essence. When the intuition weakens, pattern becomes no more than a formal design. Design as such is no more than an intellectual composition. The decay of this capacity of pattern making today is due to a loss of the intuitive faculty.

Pattern is not realistic depiction. It is a "vision" of what is reflected by the intuition. It is a product of the imagination, in the sense in which Blake used the word. Pattern is non-realistic. It may be called irrational. In a sense, it is an exaggeration. Pattern is not a scientific rendering of the original. Everyone knows that a bamboo grass pattern shows a plant that never could be. The pattern is a symbol of the plant, not the plant itself. It is an emblem of the bamboo, and yet the living bamboo is there in it. A pattern is a picture of the essence of an object, an object's very life; its beauty is of that life. In fact, it would be truer to say that its beauty is that life staring the pattern maker in the face. A pattern may lie on a table inert, just ink on paper, but it is the child of vision. Springing thus from life it must itself be alive or it is nothing. From the bamboo leaf to the pattern there is a transformation, as from chrysalis to butterfly, taking life with it into a new form. This metamorphosis is its significance. A good pattern is pregnant with beauty. The maker of a pattern draws the essence of the thing seen with his own heartbeat, life to life.

Since pattern is a portrayal of essence, all non-essentials must be stripped away; the pattern is what remains. There is no wordy explanation. There must be the "speech without words" of Zen. Good patterns are simple; if they are cluttered, they are not yet patterns.

The kind of pattern I am speaking of is not primarily decorative; it comes of Zen emptiness, of *mu* ("void"), of "thusness". The more the significance contained in a pattern, the more its vitality. In its placidity there must be movement; it lives in that no-man's-land where eloquence and silence are one. Without both it dies.

How is it that one sees the bamboo in the pattern? Because the essence of bamboo is there, just as prolonged boiling renders a concentrated flavour. The process of making a pattern out of raw material is similar, it is an extract, so when we look at a good pattern we perceive something of greater content. No bamboo grass in nature can be more beautiful than a bamboo grass pattern. We can never see nature as more beautiful than a beautiful pattern. If we see nature as beautiful, then we are, in a sense, seeing it in patterns. Pattern is the crystallization of beauty. To understand beauty and to understand pattern are aspects of the same thing.

Thus, in all good patterns there is a reinforcing of beauty. A pattern is not merely exaggeration, but an enhancing of what is true. Without this enhancement, a pattern is not true, it lacks conviction. This is why a good pattern is frequently rather terrifying. Any pattern, if it is a good one, naturally has an element of the grotesque, since it is a reinforcing of beauty—an exaggeration, one might say, without deceit. A pattern, rather than presenting the thing as it is, is a vivid representation of what the thing could never be. Thus, though not a literal depiction, it achieves a verity that transcends realism. Pattern is the power of beauty.

Every great age of art has shown elements of the grotesque. A weak, easygoing era lacks such power. Conversely, all *true* distortion, is inseparable from pattern.

Seen in this light, it is pattern that first puts us in touch with the beauty of things; it is the transmitter of beauty. Through pattern we learn how to look at nature. Without pattern, man's view of nature would be far more vague and equivocal than it is. Pattern contains the nature of nature.

Rather than saying that pattern depends on nature, thus, it would be better to say that nature depends on pattern. Pattern is nature seen in the best light. Pattern is a summing-up of a view of nature. Via pattern we see nature at its most wondrous. In a sense, an age without good patterns is an age that does not look at nature carefully. Thus, nowhere do we contact nature more vividly than in pattern. Nature converted into pattern is far more beautiful than nature as it is given.

Why should pattern be so beautiful? It provides unlimited scope for the imagination. Pattern does not explain; it leaves things to the viewer; its beauty is determined by freedom it gives to the viewer's imagination.

Pattern may be compared to a spring of water that can be drawn on eternally. To provide a source of imagination that never dries up—that, for me, is true beauty. A beautiful pattern is always receptive to the spirit of the viewer. One never tires of looking at it. Through pattern, the world and our own hearts are made beautiful. A country without pattern is an ugly country, a country that does not care for beauty. Beauty is the transformation of the world into pattern.

Let us consider the meaning of pattern afresh. On the whole, patterns tend towards symmetry. Symmetry is a natural and inevitable principle for pattern, since it has its distant and profound origins in nature itself. In nature a basic symmetry can be observed, for example in branch, leaf, and flower. They represent order. Order means numbers, laws. Laws give a point of repose. When the thing given matures into a pattern, an order has been realized. The making of pattern involves a strict observance of principles, otherwise confusion arises and ugliness instead of beauty results. When we simplify something, we can realize how simplification involves a return to the world of numbers. Numbers are expressed in symmetry. To make symmetrical and to simplify have the same significance. Without symmetry simplification cannot be achieved. Good patterns cannot be made without observance of laws.

Pictures are often distinguished from patterns, pictures being considered a depiction of nature and patterns as human compositions. Yet the two have only parted company in comparatively modern times. In olden times, there was no "realistic painting", the birth of which marked a stage in history. And yet, I believe that any good picture, even today, is also a pattern. This idea is not current nowadays, but I believe that history will eventually bring about a return to it.

Why have painting and pattern separated? The same cause underlies the idea that divides fine art and craft: the growth of individualism. Everything to do with painting has become more and more personal. Painting avoids pattern. The craftsman is essentially a communal worker; when individualism arises, the paths of "artist" and "craftsman" diverge. Also the craftsman, as I have shown, is tied by natural laws. Our epoch is at the height of concern for individualism. Pattern, as we have seen above, obeys laws, for which reason it is impersonal. In many cases, a good pattern has become the communal property of a nation: in Japan, the pattern of plum, bamboo, and pine; in China, the arabesque; in Korea, the peach; in Egypt, the water lily; in Europe, the lion rampant—these are examples of patterns born of the people and in constant use by everybody. These are the reverse of individual productions. It is not enough to seek the sources of a good picture's beauty in the individual. Most beauty is related to laws that transcend the individual. The power of that individual is puny compared with the power of the laws. The difference between former times and ours is that the individual remained unobtrusive until recently. All once used the same patterns without any question of jealousy. The separation of picture and pattern, arts and crafts, is one of the tragedies of modern times.

Crafts are of and for the great mass of people and are made in great quantity for daily life. Expensive fine crafts for the few are not of the true character of craftsmanship, which, being for everyman, are appropriately decorated with the patterns of everyman. It is natural that craft objects should be associated with patterns that are also, in a sense, communal. Painting today is prized far more than pattern, but the time will come again when this position will be reversed and beauty that transcends the individual will come to be accorded more importance.

What is the power at work in good pattern? Pattern is a product of man's skill, the true mission of which is to turn to use the laws of nature. Thus, while pattern is in a sense an artificial product, it is not so much man-made as a technique for reducing nature to something more "natural" still. It is not a vaunting of man's humanity, but a hymn to nature's mysterious power. In a good pattern, man is faithful to laws; one detects in it a true humility. It is good to the extent that it is free of any arrogance of personality. A very strange consequence of obedience to these laws is the increased freedom that then results. The acceptance of limits produces ease of mind. One may well ask why this should happen. Some insight may be gained from examining three natural limitations that every craftsman must consider: the purpose for which a given article is used; the nature of the materials employed; the appropriate techniques. With proper attention to these three limiting factors, patterns displaying that ease of mind come into being.

Use determines the nature of pattern in the first place, otherwise the pattern will be inappropriate. Let me use as an example of what I mean the coats used by farmers daily all over Japan. They are made usually of two layers of indigo dyed cotton material, hemmed and bound together by stitching in very thick thread (Plate 26). This needlework looks like added decoration but it is nothing of the sort. Its charm is in its appropriateness to use and the strength of the stitching. The delightful patterning is incidental and utterly suitable. There is no concept of decor for its own sake. From this it should become clear that the origins of pattern are inextricably sewn into the fabric of use.

It is also correct to state that pattern emerges from the texture of raw materials. If the material is poor, pattern will suffer. This does not imply that the craftsman should not adapt his patterns to the nature of his material. How very different is the painting of patterns on lacquer from painting on pots, and textile stencil dyeing from the batik wax-resist process. To disregard these innate disciplines of raw material and to think that patterns can be put anywhere with freedom of fancy is our unrecognized modern disease. We have to learn once again how to make friends with the natural raw material from which pattern blossoms.

Real pattern is also the consequence of a series of technical processes. A pattern thought out on paper is unreliable. Pattern evolved in the work itself avoids the pitfalls of paper-thought.

The knotting or weaving of rugs presents a good example of the way in which the disciplines of process decide the character of the pattern. Mere freedom of design clearly will not do; the limitations of procedure have to be followed, both strictly and willingly, to produce good pattern.

The reason why the patterns on the thread dyed *kasuri* textiles (Plates 2, 30) of the Ryūkyū Islands are so lovely is just because these limitations have been observed with zest. [How arithmetically exacting this work is can only be imagined. The weft and warp threads are dyed in calculated, appropriate lengths and colours so that, when woven, their crossing produces the desired technique-controlled pattern.—B.L.] Such patterns would never have come into existence without this peculiar technique. As this is a time-consuming and complicated process, it has been often replaced in Japan by the shortcut of printing such patterns, but the results are utterly different. Thus it should be evident how important technique with its safety rules is to the making of good pattern.

Usefulness, material, and technique, if given their due values, automatically give us calm and friendly beauty in the crafts we use from day to day. By and large, good pattern is of communal parentage. The more so the better, and the further the disciplines of nature are accepted the better the results will be. I cannot lay sufficient stress on this last behest, for our undertaking as craftsmen is to act as humble and loyal agents of the divine will inherent in nature.

In pattern man gets a view of a mighty world transcending man. In pattern we touch on the mystery of beauty. It is a strange thing that nobody seems to have stated boldly that pattern and beauty are identical. To make something beautiful and to create a pattern are not two different things. I dare to prophesy that although people's eyes are closed at the present, this profound truth will eventually be realized.

1952

The Beauty of Irregularity

A CONSPICUOUS TREND IN MODERN art movements is the pursuit of deformation, discarding conventional form, as an expression of man's quest for freedom. In referring to this avoidance of the regular in the widest sense, I shall speak here of "asymmetrical" or "irregular".

Although the contemporary accent is on deformation, expression, in both East and West, was always achieved by departing from regular form. The term "grotesque", which has an important—rather, a solemn —significance in aesthetic history, has unfortunately been misused and debased in modern times. All true art has, somewhere, an element of the grotesque. Thus the principal of irregularity, or departing from fixed form, is not new; it is merely that it has come to be employed consciously.

Why has this powerful phenomenon appeared? The irregular is in a sense something to which all who pursue true beauty resort. But primitive art from Africa, the Americas, and the South Seas was an astonishing revelation and had a magnetic effect on artists like Picasso and Matisse. Such art, as nothing else, freely expressed the beauty of deformation, of the irregular, that they sought. This resuscitation from primitive sources surely ranks with the revelation afforded by the colour prints of Japan in the late nineteenth and early twentieth centuries.

Thus "irregular" beauty is in no sense a new mode of expression; the characteristic of modern art, rather, is the fresh look it has taken at such beauty and the conscious emphasis it has placed on it. The profound truth in this emphasis is that freedom always resolves into irregularity in the end. "Free" beauty of necessity boils down to irregular beauty.

Among the earliest people consciously to appreciate this beauty of irregularity and take it as the principle underlying their creative work were the Tea masters of Japan who lived three or four centuries ago. This becomes clear immediately if one refers to the bowls used in the Tea ceremony, not one of which fails to show irregularity somewhere. Nothing, to put it the other way round, was selected for use in the Tea ceremony if it was perfect and regular. In this sense, the great masters of Tea may be considered as very modern. The so-called literati painting of the Southern school in China, so much prized in the past here and so little in the West, is also of this order of asymmetry, and the pity is that the young painters of Japan, engrossed as they are with the arts of the West, neglect their own Oriental inheritance.

In America of late years the potters in pursuit of "free form" have made a sharp and deliberate turn towards asymmetry and deformation. But already two or three centuries ago in Japan a similar tendency and preoccupation took place in the making of Raku Tea-bowls and other wares. Also, the porcelain Tea-bowls made in Ming China to the order of Japanese Tea masters, of which many still survive, often show a deliberate irregularity that is essentially foreign to China. Such pieces are the result of conscious demand from the Japanese side and, as such, occupy a rather special place in the history of ceramics. My observation in America makes me think that most of the handmade individual craftsmen's pots now being produced are mainly influenced in their irregularity and deformation by Japanese Tea taste.

An attempt to describe this love of asymmetry in modern terms was made by Kakuzō Okakura in his *The Book of Tea*. He calls it "the art of imperfection". To a younger generation this may be easy to grasp. A glance at the implements of Tea will make this clear. The shapes are irregular, the surfaces dry or sandy, the glazes of uneven thickness; the pieces piled in the kiln remain unglazed where the pots rest upon one another; fire cracks are accepted. All these characteristics are not merely put up with, but are taken as an integral part of pot making and are therefore of potential beauty. The Tea masters found depth in this naturalness. Hence Okakura's phrase.

Why should one reject the perfect in favour of the imperfect? The precise and perfect carries no overtones, admits of no freedom; the perfect is static and regulated, cold and hard. We in our own human imperfections are repelled by the perfect, since everything is apparent from the start and there is no suggestion of the infinite. Beauty must have some room, must be associated with freedom. Freedom, indeed, *is* beauty. The love of the irregular is a sign of the basic quest for freedom.

Dissatisfied with Okakura's theory, the Buddhist aesthetician Shin'ichi Hisamatsu put forward a new idea. He says that the imperfect does not, in itself, constitute beauty, the imperfect is merely a negative concept. True beauty in the Tea ceremony must be more positive. It must go further, to the point of positively rejecting the perfect. This idea certainly goes one step further than Okakura. For example, Hisamatsu's idea of "rejecting the perfect" is well illustrated in the Raku Tea-bowls. The shape is deliberately deformed—by, for example, not using a wheel—and the surface is left rough. By such means the masters sought to give life back to beauty in the Tea ceremony. All such imperfections are now sought after and refined with deliberation. From the taste of the Tea masters, this custom spread into the design of all sorts of objects throughout Japan.

Can the beauty and truth established by the early masters of Tea be explained either by Okakura's "art of imperfection" or by Hisamatsu's standard of beauty based upon the negation of perfection as an ideal? I do not think so.

In a sense such ideas are the precursors of modern deformation and "free form". Both ideas—of imperfection as a stage on the way to perfection and of the rejection of perfection—are only relative. Beauty in the Tea ceremony does not ultimately reside in imperfection in these senses. Rather, it should be seen in terms of *musō*, the Buddhist idea of unchanging formlessness behind all phenomena. In this, there is neither acceptance nor rejection.

True beauty in Tea cannot lie either in the perfect or the imperfect, but must lie in a realm where such distinctions have ceased to exist, where the imperfect is identified with the perfect. This is the beauty that I refer to, for want of a better word, as "irregular"—irregular not in the sense of being opposed to the regular, but simply that when one does not consciously aim at either there is always a little something left unaccounted for. For this reason I cannot describe the present craze for deliberate deformation in art as a path towards true beauty.

If I turn to those things that display real beauty, my meaning may become clear. A characteristic Korean bowl made in the Yi dynasty (Plate 58) or a Chinese tea-caddy of the Sung dynasty can be described as neither perfect nor imperfect. They come out of a world that existed before this dualism began—or rather, not "before or after", but in a world where the dualism is irrelevant. Neither of them were made for any Tea-rooms, or for any aesthetic reasons, but for ordinary daily use. Their slight irregularities came by chance and not by any deliberation. Skipping of glaze or other imperfection was quite fortuitous. If one visits a Korean country pottery, the mystery attached to the beauty of imperfection in the pots is solved; the whole process of throwing, turning, glazing, and firing partakes of this easy-going naturalness, rough perhaps, but beautiful and imperfect. The making of those pots is very free—but not consciously free—and full to the brim with natural good taste.

I was favoured with a rare chance of visiting the Korean village where beautiful lathed wood objects are made. When I got there after a long, hard trip, I noticed at once by their workshop many big blocks of pine wood ready for the hand lathe. But to my great astonishment, all of them were still sap green and were by no means ready for immediate use. To my surprise, a Korean craftsman took one of them, set it in a lathe, and began forthwith to turn it. The pine block was so fresh that turning made a wet spray, which gave off a scent of resin. This perplexed me very much because it is against common sense in lathe work. So I asked the artisan, "Why do you use such green material? Cracks will come out pretty soon!"

"What does it matter?" was the calm answer. I was amazed by this Zen monklike response. I felt sweat on my forehead. Yet I dared to ask him, "How can you use something that leaks?" "Just mend it", was his simple answer.

With amazement I discovered that they mend them so artistically and beautifully that the cracked piece seems better than the perfect one. So they do not mind whether it cracks or not. Our common sense is of no use for Koreans at all. They live in a world of "thusness", not of "must or must not". Their way of making things is so natural that any man-made rule becomes meaningless. They have neither attachment to the perfect piece nor to the imperfect. At the very moment when I got their unexpected answer, I came to understand for the first time the mystery of the asymmetrical nature of Korean lathe work (Plate 37). Since they use green wood, the wares inevitably deform in drying. So this asymmetry is but a natural outcome of their state of mind, not the result of conscious choice. That is to say, their minds are free from any attachment to symmetry as well as asymmetry. The deformation of their work is the natural result of nonchalance, free from any restriction. Why does Japanese lathe work look hard and cold in comparison with Korean? Because we are attached to perfection, we want to make the perfect piece. But what is human perfection after all?

In modern art, deformation is so often emphasized and insisted upon. But what a difference from Korean deformation! The former is done purposely, the latter naturally. Korean work is but an uneventful, natural outcome of the people's state of mind, free from dualistic, man-made rules. They make their asymmetrical lathe work not because they regard asymmetrical form as beautiful or symmetrical as ugly, but because they make everything without such polarized conceptions. They are quite free from the conflict between the beautiful and the ugly. Here, deeply buried, is the mystery of the endless beauty of Korean wares. They just make what they make without any pretension.

The aim of the strenuous spiritual efforts of Zen monks is focused always on grasping "thusness", which is not yet separated into right and wrong, good and evil. The following story recorded in a book by a Zen monk may well illustrate what I want to make clear.

Once there were three people who took a walk in the country. They happened to see a man standing on a hill. One of them said, "I guess he is standing on a hill to search for lost cattle". "No", the second said, "I think he is trying to find a friend who has wandered off somewhere". Whereas the third said, "No, he is simply enjoying the summer breeze". As there was no definite conclusion, they went up the hill and asked him. "Are you searching for strayed cattle?" "No", he replied. "Are you looking for your friend?" "No," again. "Are you enjoying the cool breeze?" "No", yet again. "Then why are you standing on the hill?" "I am just standing", was the answer.

The state of mind of just being or "thusness" is not confined in any preconception.

The beauty I call "irregular", the Tea masters describe as "rough". I would call attention to the quite extraordinary perspicacity of those old Tea masters in grasping this quality so firmly. A certain love of roughness is involved, behind which lurks a hidden beauty, to which we refer in our peculiar adjectives *shibui*, *wabi*, and *sabi*. Tea-bowls are not a project of the intellect. Yet their beauty is well defined, which is why it has been referred to both as the beauty of the imperfect and the beauty that deliberately rejects the perfect. Either way, it is a beauty lurking within.

It is this beauty with inner implications that is referred to as *shibui*. It is not a beauty displayed before the viewer by its creator; creation here means, rather, making a piece that will lead the viewer to draw beauty out of it for himself. In this sense, *shibui* beauty, the beauty of the Tea ceremony, is beauty that makes an artist of the viewer.

The existence of such adjectives, the more precise meaning of which I have tried to describe elsewhere, is an indication of the unique attention that has been given in these islands to depth in matters of taste. These adjectives come out of a background of Zen thinking and have a pervasive religious flavour of modesty, restraint, and inwardness. They describe an aesthetic based upon simple naturalness and reverence. This does not imply an implacable opposition to wealth and its expression in taste so much as an emphasis upon the treasury of the humble minded. The *shibui* quality is the very skin of *mu* ("void"), its outward form. Thus it may be seen that the beauty discovered in our rooms of Tea, hiding so discreetly behind irregularity, is the very opposite of that beauty unrobed by the Greeks.

For two thousand years or more Greece has dominated European art, hence the great antithesis between East and West in matters of beauty. In the field of ceramics, Western pots are almost always decorated with pattern. The beauty of the plain pot was almost unperceived, and shapes were rooted in symmetry. The ideal of Greek beauty hardly permits of irregularity or asymmetry, for it was founded upon the symmetry of the human body. By contrast the Oriental found irregular beauty in nature outside the human form. From another angle, Western man may be said to be rational and Eastern man irrational; the scientific thinking of Europe is founded in rational thought. In the East the foundation is in the heart and its inspiration, which to the Western mind, with its emphasis upon the intellect, must appear very strange, for Eastern man jumps to his conclusions on wings of intuition, whereas Occidental man arrives at his by a steady progression of intellectual steps. From this causation, man of the West brought about the age of the machine, while the man of the East is still largely dependent upon the hand.

Being founded upon nature, the quality of beauty inculcated by the early masters in the Tea-rooms of Japan was a release into healthy normality, into a freedom without overtones of wilful artistry. The implements of Tea had no overstressed individualism about them. In that respect they were utterly different from objects made today by artist-craftsmen in search of self-expression, although there is a superficial likeness. They are different, too, from the things favoured by the later men of Tea, who had lost their freedom in the search for formulas. Such deformations as they contain were born, not made, unlike the kind of distortion that is current today. Their oddness was unplanned. Contemporary "free form" is wilful and unfree. In fact it can be said that the pursuit of freedom has led to prison gates—the prison of self.

Perhaps the best way of explaining this is by a comparison of the early and later implements of Tea. The former came from either China or, more particularly, Korea. They had an enormous influence upon Japanese taste, and Japanese craftsmen began to imitate them, mainly under the patronage of the later masters. Art historians have praised and still praise these Japanese crafts; I cannot agree. The implements of Tea made in Japan in this way cannot be compared with those from abroad. The irregularity apparent in both is in fact quite different. They are entirely different in motivation. The difference is between things born and things made. A comparison between the Korean Ido bowls and the Japanese Raku Tea-bowls is sufficient to make this quite clear. The Raku bowls were made with deliberate effort, the Korean bowls were effortless products of daily living and were not even intended for Tea. In theory the Japanese bowls might have been expected to be better, but in actuality the Korean are far better. The reason for this is clear if one considers which follows more faithfully the Zen warning to "avoid the artificial". Even in one of the most renowned Raku Tea-bowls, the famous "Fuji" by Honami Kōetsu, this forced quality of taste is not entirely eradicated. Although things made with the motive of taste may charm for a time, one gets tired of them. Raku is not really freedom but captivity, not really "absence of conceptualization" but its result.

The approach to the making of better Raku Tea-bowls would necessitate a complete reversal of thinking. Really good artists and craftsmen are aware of this dilemma, but even they have not escaped from it. To do so is immensely difficult so long as one follows the path of *jiriki* (salvation through one's own efforts) rather than the *tariki* (abandonment of attempts at self-reliance; reliance on "grace") that produced the Korean bowls. This is the only way, hard though it be, for the artist, or for the craftsman who is also an artist. In his greater range and awareness he has to strive and strive to the very end to achieve that real freedom where his path joins that of the simple, natural traditional craftsman of whom I have written so much. "Free form" activity is the equivalent of the deformed Raku Tea-bowl; both suffer from the same sickness, which has to be cured by a complete reversal of thinking. I believe that the early concept of Tea, if properly understood, contains force and truth enough to bring about this transformation. The beauty of irregularity—which in its true form is actually liberated from both regularity and irregularity— the asymmetric principle contains the seed of the highest form of beauty known to man.

1954

The Buddhist Idea of Beauty

THERE IS A TREMENDOUS DIFFERENCE between the nature of God as conceived by Christians and that of the Buddha as conceived by Buddhists. God is an absolute being, distinct from that finite being called man; God is creator, man created. It is thus a fundamental characteristic of Christian philosophy to perceive the existence of God as independent from man. Some link, consequently, is required to connect these two different entities, and this link is to be found in the person of Jesus Christ. The cross symbolizes the belief that Jesus performed his difficult task at the cost of his life.

The Buddha, on the other hand, is not a creator: as is suggested by his name, he is a man who has achieved Enlightenment. Every human being, according to Buddhism, may become a Buddha; everyone is primordially qualified to do so. Of those who have achieved Buddhahood, Shakyamuni is the perfect example; all adherents of Buddhism, therefore, aspire to follow in his footsteps. Conceiving of no god apart from man, Buddhists instead suppose the existence of the Law (Logos). Although the Law may sometimes be referred to anthropomorphically, its character is far different from that of the Christian God: the manifestation of the Law is the essential property of man. Thus, by the Buddha may be understood a man in whom the Law has been realized.

What, then, is Enlightenment? It is the state of being free from all duality. Sometimes the term "Oneness" is used, but" Non-dual Entirety" (*funi*) is a more satisfactory term because Oneness is likely to be construed as the opposite of duality and hence understood in relative terms. Buddha is the name applied to a person who has achieved this Non-duality; Buddha is not the creator as opposed to the created but rather is the whole, the integrity that is beyond any such distinction. Since the creator presupposes the created, the concept remains dualistic in nature, while Buddhahood is the "state" in which that which creates and that which is created are undifferentiated. The Undifferentiated, the Non-dual, is assumed to be the inherent nature of man; all Buddhist discipline, therefore, has as its goal the achievement of this Non-dual Entirety. To be in the Non-dual state forever is the meaning of the expression "entering into Nirvana", which is the same as "attaining Buddhahood".

Buddhism, then, is not theism, but neither would it be proper to describe it as atheism, for it perceives Law in the world where there is no opposition between existence and non-existence. Again, Buddhism is neither monotheism nor polytheism, since it does not allow the entertainment of such dualistic conceptions as "one" and "many". Although some would pronounce Buddhism to be a kind of pantheism, that too would be incorrect, because Buddhism assumes no such special entity as a God. Against this assertion the argument might be advanced that Buddhism has so many deities that the mere enumeration of their names is a difficult task: Buddhism, therefore, must be polytheistic. But this argument may be refuted by the fact that the deities are merely manifestations of the immeasurable glory of the Law: they may be likened to the beams of the sun, radiating in all directions.

In Buddhist discipline, the central problem, the problem of primary importance as well as of greatest urgency, is how to eradicate man's two most representative forms of dualism—the opposition between life and death and the opposition between one's self and others; and every effort in Buddhism is directed to the solution of this problem. Terror, suffering, conflict, enmity, resentment, lust—all these are the result of man's confinement to the dualistic world. For this reason the different Buddhist sects all teach the principle of "The Gate of the Law to the Non-dual". Different points of view and dissimilar methods of exposition have given rise to numerous Buddhist sects, but all agree in amplifying the theme of Non-dual Entirety. This inherent nature of man's may be compared to his homeland; Buddhism, then, is both nostalgic rememberance as well as the way home. The man who has found the way and succeeded in returning home may be glorified by the name of Buddha. Enlightenment becomes synonymous with the realization of Non-dual Entirety, with abiding in undifferentiated integrity.

Once there was a man seeking the way to Enlightenment who visited a priest named Kanzan. "What did you come for?" asked the priest, for that is always the first question a Buddhist priest asks. "I am puzzled", replied the man, "by the problem of life and death, so I have come to seek your instruction". The priest's answer was: "Here is a place where there is neither life nor death. You might as well go home". This may, at first, seem to be an extremely impolite and unkind reply, but the fact is that the priest was trying to make clear once and for all that the world of Buddhism is a world beyond all such dualistic distinctions as that between life and death. His answer, kindly meant, was a warning that so long as life and death are conceived of as two opposing phases of existence, truth is not to be grasped.

Another illustrative anecdote concerns the great Chinese Zen monk Kuei-shan, who sought to explain the meaning of everything by making use of the circle as a symbol. One day, while engaged in training his disciples, he drew a circle on the ground, saying: "If you step into this circle, I will strike you. If you stand outside it, I will strike you just the same. What are you going to do?" By this seeming paradox, the monk hoped to show that so long as a man persists in the dualistic realm of "in" and "out", he cannot possibly attain Buddhahood.

What, the reader may ask, has this to do with the Buddhist idea of beauty? My answer is that it is an essential preamble, for I do not propose to introduce the subject of Buddhist aesthetics, since nothing of the sort has ever been cultivated as an independent branch of learning. Nor do I intend to discuss beauty as expressed through the medium of Buddhist art. My object is to clarify what interpretation of the world of beauty is possible from the Buddhist point of view and to explain the Buddhist basis on which the nature of beauty as it is pursued in the Orient chiefly depends.

Let us look at a beautiful piece of pottery. Its provenance does not concern us. If the article is beautiful, we may say that it has achieved Buddhahood, for it is not man alone that may become a Buddha. A beautiful artifact may be defined as one that reposes peacefully where it aspires to be. A man who achieves Buddhahood has entered the realm that lies beyond that of duality; by the same token, beauty is that which has been liberated—or freed—from duality.

"Freedom" is a word that is now being used rather too carelessly, and Buddhists prefer the word *muge* (literally, "liberation", "being free from impediment"), which refers to the absence of that impediment or restriction arising from relativity. It means the state of liberation from all duality, a state where there is nothing to restrict or be restricted. Beauty, then, ought to be understood as the beauty of liberation or freedom from impediment. It should be noted that true freedom is not fettered even by the idea of freedom. In this sense, liberalism cannot be said to realize the true meaning of freedom, because it is enthralled by principle. Even less does freedom mean selfish or lawless behaviour. True freedom must mean liberation from both one's self and others: it must not be in bondage to itself nor may it be restricted by others. Everything that is beautiful is, in one sense or another, a manifestation of this sort of freedom.

If beauty is the antithesis of ugliness, however, like good and bad or high and low, then it can only be conceived of relatively; but from the Buddhists' point of view, the "beauty" that simply stands opposed to ugliness is not true beauty. It is no more than a relativistic, dualistic idea. True beauty exists in the realm where there is no distinction between the beautiful and the ugly, a realm that is described as "prior to beauty and ugliness" or as a state where "beauty and ugliness are as yet unseparated". There can be no true beauty, then, outside that realm where beauty and ugliness have not yet begun to conflict with each other. In the *Muryōju-kyō* ("Sutra of Eternal Life"), the following statement is attributed to the Buddha:

> If in the land of the Buddha there remains the distinction between the beautiful and the ugly, I do not desire to be a Buddha of such a land.

Opposition between the beautiful and the ugly is unknown in the land of the Buddha; it lies beyond any such distinction, for dualism is alien to Buddhahood: here the concept of the beautiful as opposed to the ugly as well as the ugly as opposed to the beautiful both disappear.

Beyond dualism, every object—by whomever or in whatever manner it is made—finds salvation. We need not, therefore, lie helplessly enmeshed in the conflict between the beautiful and the ugly. Once the Buddhahood beyond beauty and ugliness is attained, any work by any craftsman becomes a Buddha. In our temporal world, conflict between the beautiful and the ugly goes on incessantly and can never be finally resolved. Yet only when this resolution occurs, we are told, is everyone to be saved. Therefore we are constantly instructed to revert to the stage that precedes the distinction between beauty and ugliness, good and bad, and other apparent antitheses.

In Buddhism, this idea of the Undifferentiated plays a role of the utmost importance. Since it does not concern itself with a preference for the beautiful over the ugly but rather pertains to the realm that precedes the birth of opposition between the two, it does not permit a situation in which either the ugly or, by the same token, the beautiful exists. Here there is neither: here everything is an integrity that is unique, that is itself, that is without distinction. Here, in the Buddhist idea, is the realm where art must abide. In the words of Kabir, the Indian mystic poet (1482–1512):

> The unstruck drum of Eternity is sounded within me.
> The dance of God goes on without hands and feet.
> The Harp of God is played without fingers, it is heard without ears:
>   for He is the ear, and He is the hearer.

In this profound piece of religious poetry, Kabir is telling us that the sound of a "struck drum" would be dualistic and therefore could not constitute God's music. So long as the man who strikes the drum and the drum that is struck are two different beings, true music can never be born.

In John 7:58 there is the statement "Verily, verily, I say unto you, 'Before Abraham was, I am'." Most remarkable in this quotation is the juxtaposition of the preposition "before" and the verb "am". Clearly, this "before" is not used temporally; if it were, the verb should be "I have been", not "I am". The present tense is employed here to denote not the mere present but the Eternal Now, that Now that does not depend upon either the dualistic past or future but rather is the present that partakes of eternity. Thus, an object is truly beautiful because it belongs to the Eternal Now.

All art movements tend to the pursuit of novelty, but the true essence of beauty can exist only where the distinction between the old and the new has been eliminated. The Sung dynasty pottery of China reveals a beauty that is forever new, that is still alive today. It is like a fountainhead from which one may draw water a thousand times and still find fresh water springing forth. Its beauty belongs, in the words of Jesus, to the realm of "I am", not to that of "I have been", "I was", or "I shall be". A man who considers Sung ware to be "old-fashioned", who brands it a thing of the past, is himself superannuated. Passing time cannot affect an object that is truly beautiful. All that there is, is the Eternal Now.

Two Ways

Not a single piece of Sung ware, as everyone knows, bears the signature of its maker: the potter never signed his work, however beautiful it may have been. One explanation that has been put forward is that in those days the custom of signing a work was still unknown. The true explanation, however, may be simpler still. Sung craftsmen were not self-conscious artists, they were not learned men, they were mere craftsmen making articles for daily use; most of them were probably extremely poor and had to work hard from morning till night, most also were probably badly educated and uninformed. They were not privileged people who could choose to work only when they were in a creative mood. Yet, despite all this, potters in Korea as well as in China were able to produce objects of consummate beauty, such as Sung ware and Koryo celadons: works of art that have endured through the ages.

What is more, these works of art were apparently produced with the greatest of ease, nor were they the production of merely a few potters. There were, in fact, a great many craftsmen who could produce, each and every one of them, works of equal merit. Even highly accomplished artists nowadays find that a tremendous amount of effort and practise, of meditation and ingenuity is essential in order to create a work of real value, with the result that only a few artists of more than ordinary talent succeed. But Sung and Koryo pottery was produced by no such known and individual geniuses. Can the mystery be explained in Buddhist terms?

I think it can, for Buddhism teaches that there are two ways of becoming a Buddha: one is called the "Way of Self-Power" (self-reliance; *jiriki-dō*); the other, the "Way of Other Power" (reliance on an external power or grace; *tariki-dō*). The latter may be compared to going to sea in a sailboat; the former, to walking on land. On land one very often has to traverse rugged paths, cross muddy pools, and overcome similar obstacles, time and again getting lost, growing tired, and undergoing many other trials. For that reason, it is also called the "Way of Hardship" (*nangyō-dō*), and it is the way of artists and others who believe themselves to be possessed of greatness, who want to find it out and make use of it. To do this, they are willing to rely on their own individual strength; but only those of extraordinary calibre, or genius, can complete this arduous trip.

Obviously, not all living people can be geniuses: the number of geniuses appearing in any given generation is extremely small. Thus, there are a great many people of ordinary ability living in the world, with a few geniuses among them. Are the masses doomed to simple obliteration? Is there no salvation for them? Buddhism states very explicitly that the mass of the people may also become Buddhas. The sects that emphasize that those not endowed with genius are equally to be granted the bliss of reaching their destination are called *tariki-shū* (sects of reliance on an external power), and their way is called the "Easy Way" (*igyō-dō*), since everyone is to arrive safely and unfailingly. A ship entering harbour with swelling sails is not doing so on its own but has surrendered to the great power of the wind. In a similar way, the mass of the people, even those devoid of talents, may be carried to their goal with the help of a great external power: they complete their journey with ease. Those who take the hard way seek their own greatness; those who follow the easy way surrender themselves, reflecting on their own smallness.

The beauty of China's Sung pottery, then, is an instance of the goal attained by following the Easy Way, the way of reliance on grace. Rather than attribute the quality of work to the personal ability of the potters, we must conclude that it was the world in which they lived that not only protected them but also contributed to their success. Abundant natural resources, a long tradition, repetition of effort required for production in quantity, and the fact that the articles were being made for daily use all combined to assist the potters, who, for their part, meekly accepted those conditions with both body and soul as they spent long hours at the kilns. Should a craftsman of modest talent try to resist these forces and stand on his own two feet, he would be bound to meet with difficulty and, as a result, to lose his path or fall by the wayside before reaching his destination. Such a man has but one choice to make: he must rely submissively on a Greater Power.

It is a noteworthy fact that, when the way of grace is followed, very little difference results in the beauty of the final productions, no matter who the maker may be and no matter what it may be that he is making. What minor individual differences there may be are reduced to nothing by the external power. The opposite is true when the way of self-reliance is followed, for there the personality of the maker, his individual taste, and the nature of his talent dictate what the final result will be. Needless to say, even with Sung ware made in the way of grace, there are slight differences in the quality of individual pieces, but significantly not a single one is found to have deviated positively from the right course. Putting it in Buddhist terms, we may say that every piece of Sung ware has the look of having attained Buddhahood. What a sad comparison is made by present-day industrial design!

Another noteworthy fact is that Sung ware is not a manifestation of the individual personality of the maker: that lies submerged beneath the surface, while the article itself stands out. Sung potters were working in a world where identity is not of importance. In that world, no effort is made to express individuality through the medium of things; on the contrary, the aim is to produce things through the medium of man. The beauty created there is the beauty of artifacts, not of man. If there is beauty also on the side of man, it is assuredly the beauty of the submissiveness with which he has placed himself at the mercy of the great external power.

The fact that much Sung ware is decorated with superbly drawn pictures inevitably suggests that there must have been a large number of first-rate artists at work, for the technique of the brush strokes and the rendering of the figures are both remarkable. The further fact that we never encounter a design that may be called ugly or distasteful suggests also that many of the Sung potters themselves must have been highly gifted artists. Such conclusions would be wholly erroneous. In Tz'u-chou, for example, where this type of ware was produced in great quantity, the task of drawing pictures on pottery was almost always relegated to young boys. No famous painters of the day were hired to work for the kilns. The job was performed by boys around the age of ten, children of poor families, many of whom no doubt disliked the work and had to be forced by their parents to do it. Occasionally, as they worked, their eyes would be blinded by tears. Others of the children were probably what we would now call juvenile delinquents, quarrelsome and naughty. Most of the children were illiterate; the Chinese characters that we sometimes see written in the pictures would, then, have been meaningless to the young writers. Like all children, they laughed and sang sometimes as they worked; at other times, they fought, but, no matter what kind of children they may have been, no matter what kind of pictures or characters they drew, the result was invariably one of marvellous beauty.

Obviously, this was not because each of the children was endowed with rare talent. If the hand of genius was needed, how could such a large number of boys have drawn equally good pictures? The answer may have lain partly in the nature of the materials used, but chiefly it lay in the endless repetition that was demanded of the children. The easy use of the brush and the boldness of the composition resulted from the fact that each child had to draw the same picture hundreds of times a day. This repetition produced an amazing dexterity and a quickness of hand that must have been miraculous to watch. Hesitation had no place in it; neither had anxiety or ambition. Oblivious to all these, the children worked with total disengagement.

The repetitive monotony that today would be regarded with horror; the hard work that the young boys were forced to accept as their inevitable destiny: these two factors possessed the compensatory quality of imparting beauty to the work. The obligation to draw the same picture hundreds of times a day will make a painter forget what he is drawing; he will be liberated from the dualistic opposition of dexterity and clumsiness; no longer will he need to consider the distinction between beauty and ugliness: all that he will do is move his brush quickly and unhesitatingly, without even being aware of what he is drawing. The children of Tz'u-chou may have been thinking of chrysanthemums while drawing bamboo plants; more remarkable still, they actually drew animals they had never seen and they inscribed characters they could not read. Such factors had no inhibiting effect on them. They forgot themselves as they worked, or perhaps it would be more correct to say that they worked in a world so free they were able to forget themselves.

It was precisely here, in this submissive reliance on tradition, that the beauty of their accomplishment was promised. Tradition, the accumulation of the experience and wisdom of many generations, is what Buddhists call the Given Power—an aggregate power that in all cases transcends the individuals. Illiterate craftsmen may, as individuals, be small and weak, but, supported by this Given Power of tradition, they are able to produce work of astonishing merit with the utmost ease. The importance of tradition in the work of the craftsman can hardly be exaggerated.

Once we realize that a piece of Sung pottery is not the product of some individual genius but rather of the non-individualistic power of tradition, we understand that its beauty is not personal and there is no need, therefore, to question who its maker was. To the craftsman, tradition is both the saviour and the benefactor. When he follows it, the distinction between talented and untalented individuals all but disappears: any craftsman can unfailingly produce a beautiful work of art. But if he loses sight of the long tradition behind him, his work can only be that of a bumbling incompetent.

Tradition never asks who is enlisting its help. We have hitherto been considering only pottery, but the rule holds true for other branches of practical art as well. In Coptic textiles (Plate 27), which are one of the great marvels of textile making, we see the hands not of a small number of geniuses but of a great many unlettered women working indefatigably according to tradition. We may do well to ask ourselves how many individual artists in more recent times have been able to produce work more beautiful than Coptic textiles. We then realize that without the way of grace many beautiful objects would never have been created; to regard beauty as the prerogative of genius alone is too narrow a view.

One day, in the province of Mikawa in Japan, a woman named Osono, who had been deeply instructed in the doctrine of the Other Power, was standing in front of the temple, earnestly discussing with her friends the problem of faith. A priest, passing by, patted her on the shoulder and said, "What are you talking so intently about? We may die at any moment. How can you be so heedless?" Osono replied, "Is Buddha Amitabha ever heedless?" The priest was much impressed by her answer, for he understood that what she was saying was, in effect: "A trivial woman like me is easily distracted, but Buddha Amitabha is ever on the alert for my sake, so I feel no apprehension".

Just as Osono had surrendered herself utterly to the power of Buddha Amitabha, many craftsmen give themselves up, once and for all, to tradition. If they entertained the slightest doubt about that power, their work would come to a standstill, for they are but poor creatures, hardly worth a second thought. Yet the power of tradition enables them to accomplish great work. It is not they but tradition that bears the burden. Such craftsmen do not put their signatures to what they create, but Buddha Amitabha signs his name in large characters—although our mortal eyes cannot see it. Nevertheless, anyone who admires Sung pottery or Coptic textiles is admiring, without knowing it, the Buddha's signature. Anyone who is moved by the beauty of folkcraft is in reality being moved by the invisible power that lies beneath the surface.

NON-DUALITY IN LIFE AND ART

We have been considering the Buddhist idea of beauty through the way of grace, but there is, of course, the other way—the way of relying on oneself. This, the cultivating of one's own abilities, is the way of individual artists. Among Buddhist sects that advocate this way of attaining Enlightenment, the most typical is Zen, the doctrine of which is thoroughly individualist, commanding its disciples to discipline themselves by relying on their own powers until Enlightenment is achieved. A man who would follow this way, then, must possess—above all things—a firm will and a clear head.

The final objective of Zen Buddhists is, of course, liberation from all duality: good and evil, true and false, beautiful and ugly, one's self and others, life and death, consciousness and unconsciousness. All such dualistic forms must be discarded. Day in, day out Zen Buddhists undergo rigourous training to that end, for so long as they are trapped in the polarized world, they are unable to achieve peace of mind, to attain Buddhahood. A true artist is not one who chooses beauty in order to eliminate ugliness, he is not one who dwells in a world that distinguishes between the beautiful and the ugly, but rather he is one who has entered the realm where strife between the two cannot exist. Only in the work of a man who has attained this state of mind is there no room for encroachment by the ugly or for the kind of relative beauty that is comprehensible only as an antithesis of the ugly.

Typical of Zen catechism is the dialogue between a disciple and his master, the abbot. "What if I gazed on Buddha by whisking away dust?" asked the disciple. The abbot replied immediately, "Buddha is also dust". What did the abbot mean? Did he mean that so long as one is concerned about gazing on Buddha or whisking off dust, the Buddha he sees is as good as the dust? Or did he mean to ask how the disciple could not see Buddha amid the dust without being distracted by the latter? Considering dust ugly, we desire to do away with it so as to bring forth the beautiful Buddha beneath, but Zen monks ask us if the Buddha is not plainly before our eyes in everything.

Once the master Chao-chou was asked by a disciple, "How may we be mentally prepared for all the twelve hours?" Chao-chou replied, "Most people are employed by the twelve hours, but I employ them". Zen demands of a man that he must always be the master. Most people—labouring under the spell of the Two: self and others—are not their own masters; they are either enthralled by others or they become the slaves of themselves, of their desires, their emotions, their principles. A beautiful

137

work of art, as it is understood by Zen Buddhism, is the work of a man who is not in bondage of any kind, either to beauty and ugliness or even to himself.

> Chao-chou: "In which are you, in the light or in the dark?"
> Monk: "I am in neither".
> Chao-chou: "Are you between the two then?"
> Monk: "I am not there either".
> Chao-chou: "Then you simply dwell in the words 'neither in the light nor in the dark nor in between'?"
> Monk: "I am master of those words and employ them".
> Chao-chou: "That is the answer I wanted to hear".

The Zen admonition against remaining in duality is actually a warning not to be enslaved by it, for even if one dwells in duality one may still be free provided one is the master who employs duality. That is the freedom that Zen pursues. Beauty, from the Zen point of view, is the state of non-preoccupation, it is that which is in every respect free—dexterity not in the yoke of dexterity, clumsiness not in bondage to clumsiness. Once this state is attained, everything is beautiful; but beauty cannot exist outside it, outside the realm of freedom from impediment.

In pursuit of the pre-differentiated world, Zen monks ask such questions as: "How about the time before Bodhidharma [the first Zen patriarch] came from India to China?" or "How about an old mirror before it is polished?" or "How about a lotus blossom before it emerges from the water?" Translated to the realm of aesthetics, such questions become: "How about the time before the beautiful and the ugly were differentiated?" Art is usually, so to speak, a struggle between the beautiful and the ugly, a struggle in which the artist seeks to subjugate the ugly and bring victory to the beautiful. But this is a process that can take place only after the separation of the two. The Zen point of view warns that this struggle is not a final solution to the problem, that the artist must dwell in a world before there is beauty or ugliness, that only there is salvation to be found.

This fundamental "undifferentiated" or "unborn" state is expressed in Buddhist terms as inherent or innate or inborn nature. The distinction between beauty and ugliness is post-natal and artificial, and therefore one is constantly advised to "return to one's original state", since this means liberation from dualism. The object of Buddhist aesthetics is the clarification of the following truths:

(1) That the inherent nature of man is not dualistic; that non-dual entirety is the primordial home of us all; that the place is purity itself.

(2) That the division of things into two is merely a later event and is unnatural, that the distinction between the beautiful and the ugly is based on human delusion and is wholly artificial.

(3) That we must accordingly forsake the dualistic fallacy and return to our old home of non-duality, where our salvation is promised.

Zen looks forward, then, to the state where there is no dualistic strife, a state it describes by the words *buji* ("no event") or *bunan* ("no trouble"). What is implied by the two terms is the absence of storm, of conflict, of disease, of living with one's self nature without illusion and in complete tranquillity. Worshipping the beautiful and hating the ugly are immature; Zen admonishes us to seek the world where no such antagonism exists.

Once a disciple asked the wise old priest Nan-ch'üan, "What is the Way like?" "The everyday mind is the Way", replied Nan-ch'üan, meaning by "the everyday mind" the mind inherent to one who is buffeted by no raging waves or winds. May not the suffering of the modern artist be ascribed to his unrestrained pursuit of the extraordinary? Perhaps he would be wise to reflect more deeply on the meaning of what is ordinary.

The Korean *hakeme* pottery (see pages 170–76) was made by sweeping the leather-hard green pot with a large, coarse brush full of white clay (Plate 4). The technique is a simple one, and Korean potters employed it in an extremely casual manner; they also worked very quickly, because the white clay adheres to the pot better when so treated. Japanese artists have consciously attempted to imitate this ware, for it is often used as Tea-bowls in Japan, but have failed, where Korean craftsmen, not consciously seeking to create any particular effect, have succeeded. Here, where the craftsmen do their work as a matter of course, is "the everyday mind" of the Zen Buddhists. (At one time this was the cheapest pottery in the world.) Here is the "everyday mind" of Zen: the craftsmen work "eventlessly", whereas *hakeme* attempted by conscious artists is the product of the extraordinary mind in pursuit of beauty and is therefore by its nature "eventful". The result is that Korean work is incomparably more beautiful than Japanese. In Zen terms, Korean *hakeme* is produced prior to the formation of the concepts of beauty and ugliness, while the Japanese imitation is produced after the separation of the two. The latter, clinging as it does to the dualistic view, can in no wise excel the former. Consciousness of beauty avails little as a final arbiter for the beautiful, while nothing that is ugly can exist in the "eventless, everyday mind", for that is the state where, from the beginning, no dust can collect.

Hung-jen, the Chinese Fifth Patriarch of Zen, in attempting to select a successor from among his disciples, demanded that each should compose a poem in which he was to epitomize his idea of Buddhism. His chief disciple, accordingly, wrote on the wall of a corridor:

> This body is the Bodhi tree,
> The soul is like a bright mirror;
> Take care to keep it always clean,
> And let not dust collect on it.

Hung-jen read the poem and thought it fairly good but was not altogether satisfied. The following day he found another poem written beside the previous one:

> The Bodhi is not like the tree,
> The bright mirror is not on its stand;
> As there is nothing from the first,
> Where can the dust collect?

Much moved by the poem, Hung-jen decided that its author deserved to become his successor. This was the youthful Hui-neng, who became the Sixth Patriarch of Zen.

Zen discipline is directed toward making us realize, through various means, that in our endeavor to whisk away the dust called ugliness, we are all too likely to forget that there is waiting for us a world where dust cannot collect. Thus, we are taught that the road to Buddhahood is open to all of us, salvation for all of us is inherent. Because each of us is primordially a Buddha, we are told to remain a Buddha, not to seek to become one. If we fail, the reason is that we are hindered by the man-made dualistic distinction or by the deep-rooted ignorance that underlies it.

The idea that salvation is prepared for us before our birth is also to be found in Christian thought. Sir Thomas Browne, the seventeenth century London physician, writing in *Religio Medici*, tells us:

> I was not only before my selfe, but Adam, that is in the idea of God, and the decree of that Synod held from all Eternity. And in sense, I say, the world was before the Creation, and at an end before it had

140

a beginning; and thus was I dead before I was alive, though my grave be England, my dying place was Paradise, and Eve miscarried of me before she conceiv'd of Cain.

Once two devout Buddhists were travelling together. "What shall I do should I fall into Hell?" asked one, with a worried look. "Too late, too late!" cried the other. "Before you commit a sin, Buddha Amitabha will have saved you. How can you not be saved? Do you dare to believe that your sin will be too great for the mercy of Buddha Amitabha? Alas, too late, too late!"

The reason we can find nothing to dislike in the drawings made by children is that in them the inherent nature of man finds expression without being thwarted or frustrated. The moment children become self-conscious, their pictures degenerate. Naturally, their work is inferior to that produced by an able and mature man who, having intelligence, has gone beyond intelligence. A child's work lacks this depth. To put it another way, only a few really good pictures are produced by adult artists, because their dualistically inclined intelligence overrides their inherent nature, but if an artist follows his inherent nature (which is Buddhahood), everything he produces will be a work that has already been saved, whoever he may be and whatever may be the subject of his work. He would find it impossible to produce anything that was not beautiful. Similarly, in works created by primitive peoples many are tremendously vital, reflecting the primitive power of man. It follows, therefore, that even if a man lacks high intelligence or advanced technique, he can still produce objects that are beautiful, although they may at the same time be unskilled. The reason such objects so very often deserve our love is that in them the maker's inherent Buddhahood is revealed to the observer. It is noteworthy that both Jesus and Laotze adored the innocence of children; on a somewhat different level are Blake's *Songs of Innocence*, which are far too well known to need quoting here.

Buddhism, carrying this idea a step further, teaches that the road to salvation is prepared for everyone, from the highest to the lowest, from the greatest to the least. A man need not be wise to be saved, for everyone is to be saved as he is. Even for those poor creatures who do not deserve to be saved, Amitabha, the Buddha of Mercy, has prepared a salvation that is theirs before they commit a sin. The Christian God is also characterized by compassion and grace, but at the same time, as the Bible tells

141

us, He is a stern judge who sends the righteous to heaven and the wicked to hell. Amitabha, on the other hand, is not a judge: he is, for want of a better word, an inviter, one who summons everybody without exception to come as he is into the Pure Land, having no fears because of the distinction between wise and foolish, skilful and unskilled, and the like. He prefers everyone to come naked and empty-handed, for that is the state leading directly to salvation. A priest, having produced an object, said to another, "Take this without your hands". The other promptly replied, "Give it to me without your hands". To be handless is to live in the land of the Buddha.

NON-DUALISTIC AND DUALISTIC CRAFTS

During the long Yi dynasty (1392–1910), the Koreans produced many interesting kinds of pottery (Plates 1, 4, 63–65). Regrettably, they are relatively little known as compared with the earlier, and far more famous, Koryo dynasty celadon ware. They are more naïve than celadon, simpler, rougher, and at the same time healthier. The designs drawn on them are sometimes so crude and primitive that they might have been done by children. Indeed, one may rightly call them childish—but, strangely or not, they are beautiful just as they are.

Drawn obviously without the least knowledge of technique, the designs are rich in an indescribable, an inexplicable, flavour; however casual they are, they are invariably beautiful. There is no trace of intellectual consciousness in them, no artfulness, no hesitation or perplexity. As we study Yi pottery, we discover that its beauty is not that which is attained by eliminating ugliness but rather that which bursts out before the duality even occurs to man. The pottery is not the result of a knowledge of the nature of beauty but is produced before there is any question of knowing or not knowing. To apply to it, therefore, the criterions of beauty and ugliness, skill and awkwardness, and the like makes no sense. Indeed, Yi pottery renders all critical comment meaningless. The pieces assume no pretensions, they are simply *there*, in all their naturalness, looking as if they would like to say to ingenious modern artists, "There is nothing we want. Come and join us. Everybody will be saved". They belong to a world that is singularly pure and immaculate and free from dust; perhaps there is no place in it where dust can collect. The problem of ugliness is unknown in the world of Yi pottery.

How does it happen, then, that we cannot easily produce works of equal beauty? Buddhists would say the answer lies in the fact that our minds are bound by obsession, by some attachment that deprives us of freedom; most particularly it is our enslavement to the ego that forces us into thralldom and binds us to duality. The favourite Buddhist admonition—"Give up your own self"—clearly expresses the means by which the root of duality must be torn out. But since this is not so easily done as said, our existence usually remains trammeled to obsession, from which it cannot escape.

Yi potters, however, had nothing to be attached to. They had little learning and no high-flown theories; they had no thought of seeing their work displayed at exhibitions or sold at inflated prices; nor did they look upon their products as works of art. Their commonplace and matter-of-fact attitude was what brought salvation to beauty. Yi pottery is immaculate because it was produced before there was any reason for impurity or shadow: it is, therefore, extremely natural. To be sure, there is a kind of beauty in the extraordinary and the unnatural, but these do not constitute a realm where a man may abide peacefully and contentedly. There is always an awareness of morbidity. Only an object that is natural and wholesome manifests the truest beauty, and this "natural beauty" is the Buddhist ideal. Objects that reveal ambition, objects in which lack of taste is knowingly simulated, objects where some quality such as strength or cleverness is exaggerated—these will not be universally admired for long, although they may create a momentary furor.

The fact that, in general, practical objects of wholesome and natural beauty are those intended for daily use suggests that it is this particular circumstance that imparts those qualities to them. Just as men who work hard are usually healthy, so objects that fulfill the daily functions of life are necessarily wholesome. Conversely, a lack of strength and sanity usually characterizes objects that are excessively embellished or too complicated in form, since they are unfit for daily use.

Utility does not permit unsoundness or frailty, for between use and beauty there is a close relation. Utility demands faithfulness in objects; it does not condone human self-indulgence. In creating an object intended for practical use, the maker does not push himself to the foreground or even, for that matter, to the surface. With such objects, self-assertion and error—if present at all—are reduced to a minimum. This may be one reason why useful goods are beautiful. Objects whose makers remain anon-

143

ymous have, it seems to me, an easy access to beauty; the fact that the finest examples of functional art existing in the world are mostly those that have had no opportunity to be marked by the maker's signature is worthy of very careful consideration.

Most useful objects of the present day are too superficial to answer our daily inner need: they are the victims of the commercialism that characterizes the contemporary artistic world, for commercialism is the enemy of man, extirpating all beauty from his culture. This disaster has become so widespread that a number of awakened people are seeking to counter it by working with their own hands. This is the *raison d'être* for individualism in art. But since all artists are men of aesthetic sensibility, they necessarily dwell in a world where beauty has already been separated from ugliness; thus, they are heavily burdened from the start. To reach their goal they must overcome great perils, correct gross errors, and endure extreme hardships.

Zen monks seek, through religion, to accomplish this, to realize, while abiding in duality, the state of mind that is not in bondage to duality. Artists, we may say, ate of the fruit of the forbidden tree when they divided beauty from ugliness—and for that offense were sent into the hell of duality. Should they remain where they have fallen, they will never be able to rid themselves of suffering and delusion. Meanwhile, the fact that they did fall cannot be undone. Their task, then, while remaining in the world where beauty and ugliness have been separated, is to live nonetheless a life that is not in bondage to that duality. To this end, Zen monks would tell them that they must perceive a world where "two" is "not-two" and "not-two" is "two". The starting point of Zen discipline, thus, is meditation on the question "What is Non-dualism?" Since meditation also is dualistic, however, the sole course open to the artist is to stand face-to-face with Non-dualism itself—and that means becoming a Buddha, for Buddha is no other than an incarnation of Non-dualism.

Becoming a Buddha does not mean that a man goes to the Buddha who exists apart from him but that he enters a world where there is no distinction between him and the Buddha. Buddha, thus, is in no opposition; Buddha cannot be objectified; until a man becomes one with Buddha, he cannot see Buddha; he must, in a word, enter the realm where Subject is Object. In Japanese Buddhist writing, the word *soku* is frequently encountered. In fact, one may say that the whole truth of Buddhism revolves around this single word. It defies translation; roughly, it means "namely" or "viz.". It is a connective directly or *im-mediately* identifying "two" with "not-two", "not-two" with "two".

Once a well-known Zen monk named Ma-tsu was sitting in contemplation when his teacher, Nan-yüeh, asked him what he was doing. "I am practising Zen contemplation", Ma-tsu replied. "Why?" asked Nan-yüeh. Ma-tsu answered: "Because I wish to become a Buddha". At this point Nan-yüeh picked up a piece of broken tile from the ground and began to polish it. Then the following conversation took place:

> Ma-tsu: "Master, what are you going to make?"
> Nan-yüeh: "A mirror".
> Ma-tsu: "But you cannot make a mirror out of a tile by polishing it, can you?"
> Nan-yüeh: "Nor can you become a Buddha by Zen contemplation".

What Nan-yüeh meant was that the intention of becoming a Buddha through Zen contemplation presupposes a separation between one's self and the Buddha, the objectification of the Buddha: it is, therefore, the wrong starting point. So long as Zen contemplation is regarded merely as an expedient, the cup of Zen never runs dry; but contemplation for the sake of something else is not true contemplation. Unless the act becomes an act of the Buddha himself, contemplation will be of no avail whatever; the problem cannot be solved so long as contemplation and the Buddha are two different things.

This concept may be validly applied to the world of beauty. We human beings are accustomed to thinking, "I am now painting a picture" or "I am now weaving cloth". According to Buddhism, however, such phrases express a dualistic relationship from which no true picture or cloth can result. Buddhism says that the root of the dualism is the word "I" and that it must vanish, until the stage where "picture draws picture" or "cloth weaves cloth" is reached. In one of the Buddhist scriptures is the phrase "Buddha with Buddha", which may be taken to mean "from Buddha to Buddha", and that in turn means that all true actions take place between Buddha and Buddha. Instead of man turning to Buddha or Buddha to man, Buddha turns to Buddha, all distinction or opposition between Buddha and man having disappeared. Put in another way, one may say that "the thing turns to the thing itself".

We speak of "offering prayers to God"—but true prayers are not those offered my man to God, they are, so to speak, God's voice whispered to God himself. Plotinus, the most religious minded of Greek philosophers, concluded the *Enneads* with the words, "Flight of the Alone to the Alone", a phrase of remarkable depth. Would it not be possible, then, to say that all beautiful work is work done by the work itself? When an artist creates a work, he and the work are two different things. Only when he becomes the work itself and creates the work (in other words, when the work alone is creating the whole work) does true work become possible. Not the artist but the work should say "I am": when this state is reached, a work of art deserving the name has been produced.

Meister Eckhart, the medieval German mystic, said, "The words 'I am' none can truly speak but God alone". It is not I who see God but God seeing himself in me. In Buddhist terms, all true work consists of the communion between Buddha and Buddha. To quote from a Sufi poem:

> When my beloved appears,
> With what eye do I see Him?
> With His eye, not with mine,
> For none sees Him except Himself.

To quote once again, this time from the Diamond Sutra:

> There should be nowhere to live,
> And in the nowhere thought should be born.

The nowhere in which I dwell is the abode of the Buddha, and the moment during which I do nothing is the moment when tremendous activity takes place. Buddhism describes this by means of the phrases "Abode of no dwelling" and "Mind of no thinking".

There is another Japanese Buddhist phrase that, although hard to translate, is not difficult to understand by means of example. The phrase is *fusoku furi*, which may be rendered in English as "unattached and undetached". An example would be the way the Buddha's eyes are usually depicted in Buddhist painting as neither quite open nor quite closed, suggesting the features in contemplation. The intention is to betoken what lies beyond duality. One reason for the enormous popularity of Leonardo's portrait of the woman known as Mona Lisa is that her mouth is represented as neither quite open nor quite closed. I am not suggesting that a picture in which the eyes are plainly open or closed cannot be a great picture, but what I do say is that a more profound beauty results when they are represented as being open and yet not open, closed and yet not closed.

The great charm of Sung pottery arises from the treatment of the glaze, which has melted and yet is not melted, not melted and yet melted. This, in Buddhist phraseology, is the beauty of the Mean, although this Buddhist Mean must not be understood as that which lies midway between dualistic extremes: what it signifies is that the centre is everywhere, the circumference nowhere.

SHIBUSA

Intimately associated with the Zen Buddhist idea of beauty is the Japanese Way of Tea, which does not, of course, consist simply of drinking tea but seeks to plumb to the depths the meaning of beauty. The choice of utensils, the successive stages of preparation, the etiquette of drinking, the structure and decoration of the room, the arrangement of the gardens—these, as well as other visible forms, are the agents used in the pursuit, the aim of which is not merely appreciation but rather the experiencing of beauty in the midst of daily life, not merely seeing but also acting. The Tea ceremony pursues the dynamic rather than the static aspect of beauty; it seeks beauty in the motion of things. During its four hundred years of existence, it has played a vital role in developing the aesthetic sense of the people who have taken part in it.

Further, it has always been closely related to religion, in particular to Zen Buddhism. The actual meaning of the character "Zen" is "contemplation", and in the end learning Zen and learning Tea came to have much the same significance. The Tea ceremony was, as it were, an aesthetic manifestation of Zen or a way of practising Zen in the world of beauty, and a Tea master might have been called a Zen monk living in the world of beauty. Not all students of Tea may have been aware of this, but that its spirit should be identical with the spirit of Zen has been the ideal of the ceremony.

I do not propose to go into the history or technique of Tea, but there are two aspects of it that I consider to be of some interest at this point. One is the fact that the ceremony aroused in the minds of its followers a keen interest in the utensils employed, an interest that eventually transcended the utensils required for the making and drinking of tea and was extended to functional art objects in general. It is worthy of note that the utensils employed in Tea, although they were objects of daily use, came to command the same respect and affection as paintings and pieces of sculpture.

At the same time, painting and sculpture served the practical purpose of contributing to the decoration of the room in which the ceremony was held. A painting would not be hung, for example, without first having undergone the elaborate process of mounting. Thus, one may say that in the Tea-house even painting was treated as an example of functional art.

Further, Tea taught people to look at and handle utilitarian objects more carefully than they had before, and it inspired in them a deeper interest and greater respect for those objects. It is in large measure responsible for the Japanese passion for earthenware, a passion that continues to exist and that is perhaps unique in the world in its intensity. Love of pottery is almost universal, there are a large number of collectors and frequent exhibitions, and many books on pottery and porcelain are published every year. The fact that the Japanese are such enthusiastic admirers of pottery makes the craft an easy one to follow, since well-deserved praise is granted to good potters, but the fact that a huge quantity of pottery is purchased yearly has the undesirable side effect of permitting potters of dubious merit to earn a reputation, or at any rate a living.

The second point in regard to Tea is that it formulated criteria for recognizing beauty at its height—and that not idealistically but through such concrete features as form, colour, and design. Many words were invented to describe the beauty that was to be the final criterion, and of them all perhaps the most suggestive is the adjective *shibui* (with the noun *shibusa*), for which there is no exact English counterpart. Nearest to it, perhaps, are such adjectives as "austere", "subdued", and "restrained", but to the Japanese the word is more complex, suggesting quietness, depth, simplicity, and purity. The beauty it describes is introversive, the beauty of the inner radiance. Another way of approaching its meaning is to consider its antonyms: "showy", "gaudy", "boastful", and "vulgar".

When it comes to color, *shibusa* tends toward a plain monochrome of some tranquil and unobtrusive hue, such as black, brown, or soft white; in form, something simple and peaceful; if it is decorated, only a few strokes of the brush. Reticence is an essential element in *shibusa*, but it must not be negative, it must express an infinite affirmation. An object ought, in the spirit of Buddhism, to show motion in stability, stability in motion. This reticence, which is sometimes referred to as "silence like thunder", is probably paralleled by the "eloquent silence" of medieval Christian theologians.

The word *shibusa* is in everyday use in Japan, and the criterion it sets up is taken as a measure to determine the depth or shallowness of the beauty of any given object. Interestingly enough, someone whose taste runs to the showy is aware that *shibusa* is infinitely more desirable and he looks upon it with respect, hoping that he will be able to understand it when his mind becomes more mature. Western visitors to Japan who demonstrate a preference for the beauty of *shibusa* will be esteemed by the Japanese and spoken of as people capable of understanding what beauty means in the East.

This same reticence—this *shibusa*—characterizes much of Japanese poetry and dancing as well as the school of painting known in Japan as *nanga*. Painting of this school is usually characterized by the exclusive use of black (which may be described either as a colourless colour or an all-inclusive colour) and by extreme simplicity of style, the result of the boiling away of all complexity. Very often large areas of blank space are present; such space is not empty, but implies and suggests something immeasurably large. Deeply imbued with the philosophy of Buddhism, *nanga* inevitably subscribes to the criterion of *shibusa*, a vital part of the inheritance of the Japanese, nurtured by Buddhism and disseminated by Tea.

It is noteworthy that the most treasured Tea-bowls today, those selected by early Tea masters, are almost all examples of folkcraft. They were the cheapest ware of their day, having naturally little or no decoration, and of course they were unsigned. They were monochromatic, simple in every way, intended merely for miscellaneous daily use, not even for use as Tea-bowls. None, in fact, at the time it was made, had any connection with Tea at all; strangely enough, the early Tea masters chose not a single piece that was made in order to be appreciated. It is only in more recent time that Tea-bowls, signed by their makers, were created primarily for the purpose of connoisseurship; they fail, however, to surpass the beauty of the earlier, unsigned works.

In them, the early Tea masters perceived what may be termed the virtue of poverty. This, in all religions, has played a profound spiritual role. In Christianity its finest presentation is in the teachings of St. Francis of Assisi, who preached the virtue of "Holy Poverty" and founded his mendicant order on the basis of it. Poverty, as perceived by religion, does not of course refer only to an absence of money: as is demonstrated by the declaration "Blessed are the poor in spirit", it means also humbleness of mind and the foreswearing of worldly desires. Yet this is by no means a merely negative mode of living; in Carlyle's words, it is the wisdom of the Everlasting Nay leading to the Everlasting Yea. In this sense, poverty in the present world will mean richness in the world of God. Virtually the same is Buddhism's "philosophy of emptiness", which urges the renunciation of all dualistic opposition and characterizes this sphere of nothingness by the name of "poverty". To quote a famous poem by the Zen monk Hsiang-yen:

> Last year's poverty was not yet true poverty.
> This year's poverty is at last true poverty.
> Last year there was nowhere to place the gimlet.
> This year the gimlet itself is gone.

The spirit of poverty, as revealed in the world of beauty, is what we call *shibusa*; it is the humility that may be described as subdued, austere, and restrained, and the "poverty" itself as plain, simple, and serene. The old Tea masters found the truest beauty in folkcraft because these objects, being simple and unpretentious, partook automatically of the virtues of poverty. *Shibusa* expresses the beauty of poverty: objects that fail to express it are not fit to be good Tea-bowls. The deepest beauty is suggestive of infinite potentiality rather than being merely explanatory. When taste becomes mature, it prefers plain monochromes and tranquil objects. Some may say that this is the taste of old age, and in a sense it is, for, preferring a profounder beauty, it is not easily understood by the young.

All works of art, it may be said, are more beautiful when they suggest something beyond themselves than when they end up being merely what they are. For that reason objects that were considered "complete" were not used as Tea-bowls: having shown all that they are and having nothing further to suggest, they give an impression of rigidity and coldness. That by far the greater number of Tea-bowls are of stoneware or earthenware and that very few are of porcelain may be explained by the fact that porcelain objects are in most cases too complete to be rich in after-flavour.

Recently, in the world of art, there has been apparent a remarkable tendency to attach importance to deformation. Now, although I am not personally drawn to works in which distortion is purposely attempted, I believe that truly beautiful objects usually contain in them some element of irregularity. From that point of view, it might be maintained that the grotesque is an essential ingredient of true art. An age that will tolerate grotesque art is usually a great age—but this grotesqueness must be rooted in inevitability; if contrived or strained, it can result only in unwholesomeness. True grotesque art must be healthy; conversely, sentimental art can never be great art.

If the Aphrodite of Melos were complete, with both her arms, she would probably not have been awarded the place of honour that she now holds in a great hall of the Louvre: the fact that the arms are lacking only adds to her beauty. The same principle holds true of many ruined sites, which are beautiful as they are—incomplete but eloquently poetic.

The strong hold this quest for beauty had over the early Tea masters is vividly illustrated by an anecdote so perfect one is tempted to doubt its authenticity. Yet if it is not true, it ought to be. It concerns Takeno Jōō, one of the early masters of Tea, and his disciple Sen no Rikyū, who was destined to become more famous than his master. One day the two men, walking down the street together, happened to pass an antique shop. Jōō's eyes were arrested by a beautiful vase, which, he decided after a moment, would have been more beautiful still if it lacked one of its handles. He was eager to buy it but, fearing that Rikyū might also desire to have it, said nothing. As the two men continued on their way, he decided to return to the shop alone the next day. Early the following morning he received an invitation from Rikyū, who wrote that he wanted to hold a morning Tea ceremony with a magnificent piece of pottery that he had recently acquired. At this Jōō had an inspiration and, pocketing a hammer, went off to the ceremony. Upon entering Rikyū's Tea-room, he saw a vase with flowers arranged in it. He at once recognized it as the same one he had seen in the shop the day before—and was very happy to find that the vase had already been deprived of one of its handles. That morning's Tea was a great success.

Unlike other collectors, most Tea masters prefer the incomplete; they look for slight scars or irregularities of form. If carried to excess, this desire will, of course, become unhealthy, but that there is a close relation between beauty and deformation cannot be denied. Beauty dislikes being captive to perfection. That which is profound never lends itself to logical explanation: it involves endless mystery. Contemporary Japanese potters sometimes produce pieces that are purposely deformed, but these are products of conscious artificiality and merely reflect one unfortunate aspect of the influence of Tea. True deformation in Tea-bowls results only from what is inevitable: it is wholly free from both regularity and deformity. Here again, one may say that true beauty is beauty untroubled by dualism: only the beauty of Non-dual Entirety can be true.

151

THE SENSE OF BEAUTY

Having attempted to define, from the Buddhist point of view, the essential nature of beauty and the factors that combine to render an object beautiful, I should now like to consider briefly how best to reach an understanding of that beauty—how, in other words, to appreciate it. One of the most famous among modern writers on the subject is the German philosopher Theodor Lipps, who died in 1914. Propounding a theory of empathy (*Einfühlungstheorie*), he explains that an awareness of beauty arises from the transference of one's self into the object seen and from the resulting consciousness of a fusion between the artist and his guest. In this way, Lipps says, it becomes possible for a man to understand the feeling that the object has to communicate.

Lipps's explanation presupposes a distinction between the subject that sees and the object that is seen and does not go beyond the intercourse between the two; his theory, then, stands solidly on a dualistic base and therefore cannot, according to Buddhism, provide the means for a full comprehension of beauty. The sense of beauty is born when the opposition between subject and object has been dissolved, when the subject called "I" and the object called "it" have both vanished into the realm of Non-dual Entirety, when there is no longer anybody to transfer or anything to be transferred. Neither the "I" that faces "it" nor the "it" that faces the "I" can attain reality. A true awareness of beauty is to be found where beauty watches beauty, not where "I" watch "it". The "I-it" relationship cannot reveal beauty in its entirety, but only a small part of it. Zen Buddhism uses the phrase *kenshō*, in which *ken* means "seeing" and *shō* "nature"; taken together, however, the two words do not mean "seeing nature" but rather "seeing into one's nature". In *kenshō* the artist and his guest are not two distinguishable concepts.

Just as Rome was once the great metropolis of Europe, so that of ancient China was the city of Chang-an, which every Chinese of the time longed to visit. "To everybody is given the way to Chang-an", said a monk to his teacher, "now how can I go there?" The master answered at once: "Where are you right now?" Where is Chang-an? how may I reach it? how long does the journey take?—in questions such as these Chang-an is not to be found. What the master meant was that the town of spirit cannot exist except *at this very instant*, an instant without past or future, and *on this very spot*, a spot without right or left.

Another illustrative anecdote concerns a monk who for long had been living away from the society of men in a hut in remote mountains. One day a visitor who had found his way there asked him, "How many years have you been living here?" The monk replied simply, "There are no days on the calendar in these mountains". A man who lives where time can be measured on a clock is living in a secular world; a monk should live in a world where there is neither passage of time nor length of time. He should live a life that is not measured by the calendar. A sense of beauty, similarly, is timeless: it may be said to exist *at this very instant*, unbounded by past or future, and a beautiful object may be said to exist *on this very spot*, unbounded by right or left.

When I am asked for a Buddhist explanation of the perception of beauty, my answer is a simple one: "One must discard one's self". But of course the process is not easily accomplished; grasping the reality of beauty is no easier. In looking at objects, a man makes use of this intelligence; he evaluates on the basis of his own conceptions, he passes judgement on the basis of his own experience. In so doing, "I" become the master pronouncing on the "object", which I regard as my guest. Since one's self does not disappear in this process, "I" and "it" remain two different entities; no union between the two occurs.

The lingering on of the self may be likened to looking through coloured spectacles: one is gazing at objects through the colour called ego and therefore one cannot see them as they are, one can only see them enveloped in something else. Often a man, in attempting to see things, makes use of some form of measurement, its degrees marked in accordance with his own intellect; with it he tries to appraise everything quantitatively. But many things do not permit of such treatment, so as a result he sees only those parts that do. Whenever fixed rules are applied to an object, only certain parts of it may be perceived. But an object is an integrity; when, therefore, we force dualistic distinctions upon it, its reality has already fled.

The process may be likened to that of a man trying to catch the running water of a river: once it is caught, it is no longer running. An intellectual approach is not of much value in the understanding of beauty. The *Theologia Germanica*, written in the fourteenth century, tells us: "He would know before he believeth, cometh never to true knowledge". Applied to the perception of beauty, this means that if a man employs the function of knowing before seeing, his power to see is impaired. More-

153

over, the function of seeing cannot be derived out of the function of knowing: intuition is not born of knowledge. Integrity may be subjected to analysis but may not be recovered from the analysed parts, just as a sheet of paper may be cut into many pieces but the original sheet is not restored by bringing the pieces together.

Intuition is vital to an understanding of beauty because it is the faculty that permits us to look directly at objects. In order to give free play to intuition, one must not permit anything to intervene between one's self and the object. When that happens, one's self and the object remain separated to the end and intuition can have but a limited sphere to work in, revealing only a partial view of the object. Only after one's self has been reduced to nothing can intuition wield its unrestricted power, for only then is the opposition between that which sees and that which is seen dissipated. The viewer is not restrained by subjectivity nor does the viewed end in objectivity; the subject is itself the object, and the object is itself the subject. When intuition is at work, the object is never objectified; or, in Buddhist phraseology, seeing intuitively means entering the sphere of Non-duality.

Buddhism, therefore, insists that one receive without hands, or, in more eloquent expressions, play upon the lute without strings or sound the flute without holes. For many, the sharp edge of intuition is blunted by a failure to see with the naked mind. To be naked-minded means to be unrestricted by the eyes that see. When this is achieved, even the dust that spoils the vision will have vanished.

The fact that collections of art objects are frequently of highly uneven quality, perfection standing side by side with mediocrity, is due to the fact that in the collector himself there is a quality that has blunted the intuitive acumen: it has prevented his selecting only the treasures that should properly make up his collection. The moment he begins to boast of the quantity, variety, or rarity of his collection, to seek to collect only those objects that are in perfect condition, or to bow to popular opinion, he has subjected himself to bonds that deprive his faculty of intuition, of its freedom to operate. He ceases to receive objects without using his hands, his attitude becomes restricted, beauty no longer reveals to him its own reality. He will then be seduced into believing the ugly to be beautiful and into refusing to accept as beautiful what is actually beautiful. Collectors are prone to such frailties whenever they fail to allow intuition to function at the height of its power.

First impressions, as is well known, are often astonishingly sound, and that is because we are so constituted as to perceive others with living eyes and to see objects with fresh perception. In first impressions, the faculty of intuition functions most freely, permitting us to look at unfamiliar objects with ever new and living perception. With familiar objects the process becomes increasingly less functional, but that of course is only because our own sense of perception has become dulled, not because the intrinsic value of the objects has lessened. A man of intuition is one capable of always deriving fresh impressions from objects. Intuition is the power of seeing *at this very moment*.

Once there was a man named Kichibei, whose unfortunate wife had been bed-ridden for two years. He himself swept the house every day, cooked all the meals, and washed the clothes. When a compassionate villager remarked how tiring all this must be, he replied, "I do not know what fatigue is, because caring for my wife every day is always both a first experience and a last experience. There is no doing it again, and so I never tire of it". Kichibei, then, lived always in the immediate moment, in "the right now". Indeed, living in "the right now" is the true condition of man's being, and when he looks at objects in "the right now", beauty will never conceal itself from him—for intuition means nothing more or less than "seeing right now". A man of intuition may be defined as one who allows impressions to be forever new: from this point of view, an object of art is created by those who look at it, and a man of intuition is an able artist.

Why do we long for beauty? The Buddhists would reply that the world of beauty is our home and that we are born with a love for home. To long for beauty, therefore, is the same as to long for home. But home, as we know, is the world of Non-dual Entirety: everything that has been divided yearns to be reunited; everything has, so to speak, been divided in order to long to be one again. Regarding a beautiful object, then, is the same as looking at one's own native home; put another way, it is the same as looking at the original condition of man himself. He who buys a beautiful object is in reality buying himself, and he who looks at a beautiful object is seeing in it his primordial self. In an ardent lover of Sung pottery, the pottery recognizes its own home; conversely, the lover recovers his home in the pottery. Here the viewer and the viewed are not two entities.

155

EAST AND WEST

There is another matter that may lie within the realm of beauty. It is a truism to say that most men desire peace and loathe war; it is equally a truism to note that peace is not easily attained. Is it enough to say that war is a punishment for sin, a punishment that winner and loser share alike? More immediate, perhaps, is the fact that man tries to solve his differences by political means, always taking into first consideration the advantage that might accrue to his own country. Under such circumstances, is not war inevitable?

I believe, however, that it is possible for man to break through national barriers, and I believe further that it is in the realm of beauty that he may most easily accomplish this. True, even in the world of art, disputes arise out of opposing theories and principles; nevertheless, a beautiful object is undeniably beautiful and by its universal appeal has the power—at least temporarily—to make people forget their selfish nationalism. It is one of the virtues of beauty that it has this power: to make one forget one's self and so put an end to strife.

Happily, each nation has in its own art an expression of its particular perception of beauty. By looking at the art of all peoples, by loving and respecting it, the nations of the world can, I believe, achieve mutual spiritual harmony. We ought, in fact, to be grateful that there are beautiful objects capable of breaking down the barriers between east and west and between north and south. Peace is broken when there is dualism and opposition; but as we know, there is a world beyond this opposition where dualism is eliminated, and there must be a connecting road. I do not suggest that East and West should be made monochromatic; they should remain polychromatic but without falling into polychromatic feuds. This realm of harmony is man's true abode; but seeking it only in either East or West is inadequate and a most unfortunate decision for him to make.

One day, a Zen abbot saw a disciple about to leave the temple.

> Abbot: "Where are you going?"
> Disciple: "I am going to my home in the west".
> Abbot: "I want to invite you to the house in the east. Will you come?"
> Disciple: "I am afraid I cannot".
> Abbot: "In that case, your abode is not yet fixed".

A man of the west, the abbot is saying, may do well to make the west his home, but so long as he is bound to it, he will not be able to find his true home even in the west. West as opposed to east is only a dualistic west, not the west where one's spirit may abide in peace.

A final Buddhist anecdote I should like to cite here concerns Hui-neng, the sixth Zen patriarch whom we encountered earlier. While still a young man, before being accepted as a disciple, he was subjected to an examination by the Zen master, Hung-jen. The questions and answers are as follows:

Hung-jen: "What did you come for?"
Hui-neng: "I came to learn Buddhism".
Hung-jen: "Where did you come from?"
Hui-neng: "I came from the south".
Hung-jen: "Men of the south are all like apes—they cannot understand Buddhism. Go away at once".
Hui-neng: "There may be a north and a south on land, but there can be neither in Buddhahood".

He was immediately accepted. North and south, he was saying, east and west: they are two and yet not two. I believe that if we can ever accept this, we can hope for no greater beatitude. The discipline of aesthetics finds its chief reason for existence in putting forth this fundamental truth.

1952

Crafts of Okinawa

IF ONE OPENS AN ATLAS, there islands may be found strung out in a line between the southernmost of the four main Japanese islands and Taiwan. The largest is called by its Japanese name, Okinawa, which means "Offshore Rope," describing its shape. The old Chinese name for the islands is Liu Ch'iu, Ryūkyū being the Japanese pronunciation of the same characters.

The climate is semi-tropical and damp, and the islands are subject to devastating typhoons coming up the coast of China from the Philippines. The land is verdant, and flowers bloom throughout the year. Trees grow well, and include many unusual varieties, and there are a considerable number of large pine and bamboo groves. Fish, shellfish, and insects abound. It is a paradise for naturalists. The islands are fringed with green waters covering coral.

The main island, Okinawa, is about ninety miles long and mountainous in the north. The scenery is very beautiful, particularly in the south, where there are gently rolling hills and paddy fields that stretch down to the sea. The capital is the city of Naha, and not far from it are the remains of the palace of the former kings, where the cultural activities—the architecture and sculpture, literature and music, dancing and the decorative arts—of this ancient, and formerly semi-independent kingdom were centred. This tiny chain of islands adrift in the ocean has had a singular and independent cultural history of one thousand years.

Although closest to Fuchien Province in China, influences came to Okinawa mainly from the north, from Japan of one thousand years ago. Language, custom, and architecture are almost entirely Japanese in

158

origin. The many suppositions that the people of Okinawa were primitive, like the aborigines of Taiwan, is a complete error due to ignorance of their true culture and to their own humility about it. It is high time that a fresh estimate of its value should be undertaken. After experiencing it with my own eyes, ears, and palate, I feel driven to write this apprecia- tion, because in company with my craftsmen friends I have been aston- ished at the high proportion of things of great beauty that we have found. For the first time I became aware of how much this island life had been neglected and needed study. Its beauty is such that it is a miracle that it remained unspoiled. Apparently nobody had recognized its loveliness before we came. The politicians had simply regarded these small islands as a burden—so poor, so backward, so unimportant.

In contrast, our belief is that the Okinawans possess a richness of artistic inheritance in arts and crafts such as to put cultural values above the economic. The question in our minds is how far this inheritance can be carried forward into the future. Instead of its reputation, hitherto, as a poverty-stricken, isolated string of islands, we want to establish its brightness to correct these misapprehensions and to give the people encouragement and self-confidence.

I have written these lines to the people of Japan with this intention and hope.

TOMBS

Any Japanese who visits the tombs of our long-dead emperors is filled with a sense of freshness and purity in the ritual sense. The religious faith of the Japanese can be summed up in the idea of purity.

I have made a journey on muleback to the tombs of the Ming emperors in northern China. I was astounded by their scale. I remember we rode miles from the gateway to the tombs themselves, with a sense of the size and power of the Chinese culture. The contrast with the Japanese em- phasis on purity is great.

In Europe I visited the medieval cathedrals where the images of the dead lie carved in marble. The tombs are monuments symbolizing the human beings themselves; what they seek to do is arouse in us personal memories of the departed. Visiting the cemeteries of the West, it is their cheerfulness that strikes one. People even go to walk there for pleasure. By contrast, Japanese cemeteries are places of eternal quiet; this desire that the dead should have eternal quiet is in part an influence of Buddhist teachings.

We visited ancient tombs at Kangso in Korea. Dating back to the time of the Koguryo kingdom, they are the product of a time when Buddhism had not yet taken a thorough hold on Korea. The wall paintings between black outlines were painted with an unearthly force of imagination that would put any modern artist to shame.

In short, it seems that the character, aspirations, and religious beliefs of a nation are best symbolized in the tombs in which its inhabitants bury their kings and emperors, their ancestors, and their fellows. In our attitudes to death, we express ourselves most truly. Faced with death, a nation confesses what is its real philosophy of life. All graves are honest and earnest expressions of a country's religious beliefs, whether what is expressed be purity, or massiveness, or brilliance, or quietude, or even desolation.

Of all the myriad graves on earth, the tombs of the old kings of Okinawa (Plate 43) are the most weird and terrifying. Nor have I seen family tombs of so fine a form. They are a direct manifestation of a vivid faith in the actual existence of spirits. Standing there, I felt the souls of the long dead speaking to me. It was borne to me that here are the mainsprings, the mysterious mainsprings, of the whole of the life of Okinawa. The faith expressed here has its roots in the most distant depths of the human spirit. Astonishingly, it goes back to a point preceding any religious teachings that might distinguish between the pure and the impure; it belongs to a realm where man was still untroubled by ideas of morality. In what modern country could one still find such vital expressions of a faith with such remote origins?

One has a sense, even, that our religions and our moralities are artificial things whose history is still short and shallow. Our thinking that troubles itself with questions of a future life is nothing more—these tombs seem to say—than a confession of the poverty of our imaginations. If spirits do not exist, then nothing exists; nothing is so splendidly and vividly alive as the spirit. And it is for the spirit to live in that tombs are built.

However humble ordinary dwellings may be, the dwellings of the spirits at least must be decent structures. The royal tombs, after all, are referred to as the "Jewelled Palace". They are not places to "enshrine" the dead or to commemorate the dead; nor again are they intended to vaunt the achievements of ancestors or to serve as places of repose for their physical remains. They are the dwellings of the spirits who, through death, have entered upon true life.

I recalled the emblazoned vulgarity of our Tokugawa Mausoleum at Nikkō. That brilliance is nothing but a vaunting of worldly prestige. What sense of spirituality could such over-elaborate decoration hope to convey? The tombs of Okinawa are on quite a different level. Even the tombs of the common people are extraordinarily fine in shape; some take the form of houses, others are in the shape of a tortoise-shell, with an extraordinary sense of volume (Plate 44).

Had the Okinawan people not really believed that these were the congregate homes of the living-dead, they could not have conceived them. The form comes from South China, but the people of the islands have made them yet more impressive and truly works of imagination representative of their culture.

Where they are gathered in one vast graveyard near Naha, the impression they give is tremendous, not only as a place of tombs, but more as a revelation of the living spirit of the dead. Without an understanding of this prime fact it would be difficult to grasp the quality of the crafts of the Ryūkyūs, because they all contain a flavour of joyful yielding of belief, which, the people—as childlike, or even primitive, country people—are unwilling to forgo. By comparison how much can we moderns with all our learning and metropolitan life seize beauty directly? Would it not be fair to say that the ugliness of our artifacts is due to loss of faith?

For anyone concerned about the relationship between the world of faith and the world of beauty there is much to be learned in Okinawa.

THE ROYAL SUBURB OF SHURI

I have visited almost all the castle towns and cities of Japan, but if anyone was to ask me which was the most beautiful, I would answer without hesitation Shuri of Okinawa (Plate 45). The moats and walls of the Imperial Palace in Tokyo, the approaches and environs of Kyoto, the temples of Nara, or the old castle of Himeji all float into my mind, but they are fragments of a whole that was and has ceased to be, and in its place are foreign buildings without overall planning, without connection with the old castle or palace, with cheap, noisy backstreets. In the race to be up-to-date there is no thought of style or preservation of fine tradition, there is no time for such fancies. For this reason there is no town in all Japan where what was fine as a whole can be found—only fragments remain. In the early Meiji period rush to absorb everything from the West the damage was done, and it is only quite recently that thought has begun to be given to preservation. Even in the old capital of Kyoto, where more is preserved than elsewhere, the new and the ugly intrude brazenly without control. If the new were good, it would be another tale. Sad to say, Japanese towns now can show very few beautiful things of which they can be proud before the world.

Shuri of Okinawa should be given first place in spite of the memories of Okinawans of a still more lovely capital city of fifty years ago. They recall, with sorrow, many old buildings, trees, walls, etc. that have been destroyed, and a population that has diminished. Despite these changes for the worse, more remains than elsewhere. Its beauty may be unrealized by its inhabitants, but to me it is a dream city. The large schools and churches in clumsy Western style are deplorable, but mercifully few. Cheap zinc roofs are still few and far between. Almost all buildings are roofed with the rich, red, old-style tiles. Towns with such a unity of style are scarcely to be found in the main islands of Japan now.

Among the houses of the city below the hill, abundant trees provide shade for all. We walked its streets in a dream. No matter which way we turned the dream held; moss grew on ancient walls, the dark green leaves threw down shade, and everywhere were those lovely red-tiled roofs with their generous white mortar pointing and grotesque pottery heraldic animals. It is a garden city, alive in the beauty of man's hands working in harmony with nature. We just wanted to continue strolling there endlessly. Such places of unified beauty are rare. In comparison, how very confused and full of ugliness the Japanese main islands have become. Under the impact of undigested foreign influences our capital city no longer expresses an indigenous culture. But Shuri still does; therefore it is our obligation to preserve it. I pray the Okinawan people themselves will do so.

ROOF TILES

One of the chief charms of Oriental buildings is their roofs. There are many kinds—gabled, hipped and gabled, etc.—but all of them feature deep eaves. Such eaves are partly dictated by the needs of wood construc-

162

tion, but in Japan, with its strong winds and heavy rains, they are also essential. The two most important elements in these roofs are the framework and the covering of tiles, boards, or thatch. Thatch gives a friendly and soft outline and silence, but the tile roof has the most strength of form. The classic style, *hon-kawarabuki*, consists of a combination of flat (actually rather curved) and rounded tiles fitted together.

Japanese tiling, however, has vastly deteriorated; straight roof lines have taken the place of curved and wave forms; overlapped tile has ousted the round, ridged tile for reasons of economy. The results are hard and thin compared with the substantiality and beauty now only to be seen in a few shrines, temples, and occasionally old homes. Some buildings use exclusively flat tiles in wave patterns. The colour has been changed as well from the old reds to cold gray. The architectural loss is great. One of the chief causes of the loss of beauty is the omission of the upward curve at both ends of the ridge, which now forms a simple straight line. Even the "devil" tiles at the ridge ends include very few good specimens.

The true beauty of tiled roofs is now only to be found in Okinawa. I cannot forget the delight with which we scanned the roofs of Naha as we approached by ship. The reds were varied and lovely, set off as they were by full and generous white pointing made from ample supplies of crushed coral. Equally attractive was the ample curve of the ridge line, which has disappeared in Japan, and the simplicity and economy of the two ends. Sometimes, too, they use decorative tiles with flower patterns at the edge of the eaves. And, here and there, strange and grotesque animals sit on each roof (Plate 48), questioning and regarding the passerby.

Such magnificent, massive, tiled roofs are not to be found anywhere else. The dark green leaves against the red-and-white roofs assured us that indeed we had entered a world of dreams. Later we visited the tile works and were dumbfounded by the simple naturalness and speed with which men's hands were turning out those tiles by ancient and elementary methods. I doubt that there is any country, with the exception of Korea, where such lovely tiles are made.

Looking down once more from the royal hill at Shuri, I reflected that the finest tiling in Japan to be seen today is on structures of the Tempyō era (729–749), such as the Sangatsu-dō and the Tōshōdai-ji at Nara. But a similar beauty is to be found everywhere in Okinawa. What have we lost? If the roofs of Naha go, half the beauty of this paradise will go with them (Plates 46, 47)

163

Music

The world's music today has become concert music. This used not to be the case when music and melody flowered from common life. The change is not for the better, for music that is separate from life is separate from nature. The atmosphere of the concert hall is not altogether admirable; those who go tend to be erudite or specialized. They go to hear a great composer or a great interpreter. The dregs are left to the man in the street. Is this good? Has the root of music not been cut? I believe that when music was alive in life there was little need for concerts and concert halls. The life of music was in the streets, the homes, and the fields.

What lit my heart was to find this in Okinawa, and in this sense I call it a land of song and dance. Not only Okinawa itself but in all the small islands, and especially in Yaeyama far to the south. Everybody sings: one starts, and at once others gather and join in, bringing their own contribution of words, turning everything they want to say into song on the spot. There is no stardom; they all sing well in work and play. This is the song of the people, folksong, a world of music before division into good and bad. There is no room for the music critic, because music is alive in all the people. The innate potential in all is uninhibited. In the countryside and in the towns there is no poisoned or vulgar song, nor any sentimentality. The songs of Okinawa are natural, direct, sincere—in a word, *shibui*.

Songs of innocence, songs of heaven. Here is the root of music—and it is different from concert music. Poetry, music, and dance may be had here from their source. They may be had separately, but they are one; there are no separate poets, composers, and choreographers. Each may be enjoyed singly, in depth, but the root is one. When combined, as here, at source, the effect is deeply moving. One of the reasons I love Okinawa is that in the world of song it still preserves the basic human qualities that we have lost.

Dance

Of the dance forms of Japan, the Nō drama, an art almost without parallel in the world, is one of the peaks of Oriental art in which the spirit of Zen is expressed. It is an ultimate expression of "movement within repose", an art in which every aspect—words, music, dance, costumes, stage—have been formalized into one fixed form. I believe Japan has cause for

164

pride in its possession of such an inheritance. At the same time this noble tradition is in no way connected with the art and life of today. It has a special value therein, for it can take us into a realm outside time but leaves us without a corresponding format for today. When we see Nō, we can enjoy ourselves in a remote world. We may be thankful for that, but would not Nō itself gain more if it sprang from our life today? The drama takes place in a world of the imagination, far off, inaccessible to the average man and woman, it has become so recondite that it is only within reach of those especially interested.

The dance forms of the Okinawan people, originating in the twelfth to fourteenth centuries, are still vivid with a modern vitality. The dances may have suffered some decay, but compared with the Nō of Japan they are an expression of continuous life. Style is completely derived from the Nō, yet it is much closer to life and has a greater immediacy. With the dances known as *kumi-odori*, even the titles are often the same as in Nō. Nō belongs to a past age; this art still springs from living hearts. People who lived in the Japan of the Ashikaga era (1333–1573) must have felt Nō drama as Okinawan dance can still be felt. It is a formal art, as is the Nō, but here form and content have a more immediate connection.

It was for such reasons that I was so astonished and delighted. Those who love Nō should come to these islands to listen to and watch song and dance, night by night, sparkling and living with an ancient vitality and grace. Everybody dances, everybody sings. The dances spring from the life of the people. The Japanese songs and dances of the Bon festival are also impressive, but less alive than these expressions of intensity of spirit. I beg you my readers to waste no time before coming to see such dance as this, whether of fishermen, or farmers, or the slow, quiet, and deep dances of the old court.

[I have visited these islands twice with Shōji Hamada and his wife. The second occasion it was as recent as 1969, and with my wife Janet.

The Okinawa capital, Naha, which Yanagi describes with such sympathy and insight, we did not find—the terrible fighting had destroyed so much life and culture, nevertheless much remains on the outskirts and in the countryside. Royal Shuri was gone. In the capital itself that dreamlike beauty of a thousand-year-old semi-independent and peaceful kingdom had almost disappeared. Yet the revival of crafts has begun; we received a wonderful reception by two to three hundred of its lovers and promoters and we feasted together—beautiful song with a lyricism of the southerly seas, graceful, undulating folk dance, and noble, ritual court dance dating back to the twelfth and thirteenth centuries. In both the folk dance and musical accompaniment of court dance I could not perceive a resemblance of Nō music. There was a possible influence from China in the court music, but what I heard was, I think, mainly the voice of South Pacific sea-girt islands. Both dance and music were clearly distinct from that of China, Korea, and Japan, and worthy of the lovely textiles; yet in the dance on one side I felt Chinese court dance resembling T'ang dynasty pottery burial figurines and on the other the footwork of Nō dance. In the gliding forward step of the former, a pause like syncopation; in the latter, a broken half stamp during the more dramatic parts in certain Nō plays. I was relieved by the ardent delight with which my intuitive guesswork regarding dance inspiration was received.

But to return to the frontal attack at the beginning of the music section. Sharp as it is and maybe offensive to some music lovers, there is no hiding the exposure of cultural sickness pervading the whole of the Western world, and not in music alone. The artist with his exhibitionism, glass cases, and fabulous prices is accused of being far from nature. It was the exhibitionism of concerts and art galleries, especially in city life, which repelled Yanagi in its artifice, not good art. For the affronted English reader, I would refer to the prophetic vision of William Blake 150 years ago. Nevertheless, even in bad periods art does emerge, even as the lotus blooms in mud.—B.L.]

Okinawan Dyeing

If one thinks of Japanese dyeing as a whole, one's mind dwells upon the tradition of *Yūzen* in all its variety of tie-dyeing, free painting, stencil, etc., as its finest flowering. So I thought, too, until I saw the *bingata* (polychrome stencil dyeing) of Okinawa. Doubtless it was influenced by the *sarasa* (cotton prints) from the south and *Yūzen* from the north, but it transcends them, a splendid combination of design, colouring, and techniques. No garments made by the womanfolk of any country exceed these in colourfulness—particularly suitable in a southern country like Okinawa—blending the gay reds, yellows, and greens of nature.

I think greater homage should be paid to *bingata* (Plate 7) than to *Yūzen* because of its more fundamental honesty. As anyone knows who has seen *Yūzen*, much hand-painting and embroidery is added to the basic weaving and dyeing; to that extent it is less pure and faithful to the dictates of material and method. *Bingata* keeps strictly to stencil technique. Batik, decorated by the wax resist process, is technically a much earlier stage. Moreover, *Yūzen* is almost entirely on silk, but *bingata* is mainly on cotton and hemp. These textiles were available to all, and were not for the upper classes alone. So many houses in the old capital of Shuri produced *bingata*, that it was the clothing material for most of its inhabitants, for special occasions at least.

A speciality of Okinawan dyes was the skilful combination of vegetable juices and metal oxides. This was scarcely due to chance discovery alone, but to the desire for colour clarity and variety on the part of the Okinawan people. In the matter of pattern, these people show an instinctive good taste. I am always astonished at their freedom; their bird or flower patterns are so easily and freshly taken from nature. Mountains, rivers, waves or buildings become patterns lovelier than nature itself casually provides, yet still more strongly evoke nature's beauty (Plate 49).

Thus we may say the Okinawan birds remind us of the patterns, and the patterns of birds. Unhappily, however, the production of these textiles has fallen off during the last thirty or forty years, and there is now only one old stencil cutter left. There are two causes for this: first, the importation of cheap Japanese goods that have a flash appeal, deceiving the Okinawan shopper; second, because, as elsewhere, they tend to underestimate their own country's things. Thus is the increment of a noble past being lost. For the Okinawan people this is a pity, for although *bingata* was only produced for clothing, many new uses could have been found for it, for example, as curtains, cushions, etc. Since the Okinawan people gave birth to such great beauty, will nobody reassess the position and revive these crafts? I pray for that day to come, and soon.

WEAVING

I keep wondering about the future of Okinawa. Politicians, in all good faith presumably, want these people to modernize and to become a more up-to-date part of Japan. These island people look towards the capital, Tokyo, with respect and desire. That is natural: they look with the provincial eyes of a former age of handwork, so it is almost inevitable that they feel they must throw aside their old ways.

But surely the matter needs more careful consideration: Evaluating a culture involves more than the question of new or old,—the basic consideration is what is true or untrue. There are so many aspects of this new civilization of which we should be ashamed. Take weaving. Our clothing is its product; it comes out of huge factories, our yarns and dyes are the product of applied science, of intellectual control of the material world, compared with which the simpler efforts of men of the age of handwork are humbled. Nevertheless what this new civilization makes is neither honest nor beautiful. How has this come about?

There are two main causes. The first is that men of the new age think that it is far more advanced than in fact it is. An honest scientist knows this full well; he knows that although mechanics seem wonderful, the instruments are in fact clumsy, limited, and puerile before the subtleties of nature. Who would say that nylon is better than silk? Secondly, the social effect of factory life: the principle of profit in industry; capitalism; profit as against quality; advertising of the cheap and poor articles to the masses. Why should the makers of the splendid crafts of the Ryūkyūs bow down in humility before these gods? I feel this the more strongly because the possibility still remains that they may not do so.

The most unique and beautiful weaving in Okinawa is that called *kasuri* (Plate 2), similar to the Indonesian *ikat* except that either warp, weft, or both are dyed in measured lengths before weaving. This technique is much employed in Japan, but by far the best *kasuri* was made in Okinawa. Their coloured *kasuri*, in particular, has no rival. Okinawan *kasuri* technique probably traces its origins as far as India, and would seem to have reached the Ryūkyūs via the islands that dot the Pacific to the south. In Japan it was developed into picture patterns, but again the product of the islands is purest and best. They did not confine themselves to blue and white, but produced many coloured *kasuri* of incomparable beauty. They also combined it with attractive striped weaves.

Besides Shuri and other parts of the main island, *kasuri* was produced in many of the smaller islands composing the Ryūkyūs. As far as this technique is concerned, they were the teachers of the Japanese. But many of the Japanese products, such as *Ōshima-gasuri* and *Satsuma-jōfu*, by comparison are over-refined and over-skilful. The Okinawan products are of stronger, better craftsmanship. *Kasuri* weaving is by no means the only unique technique; the variety is so great that it may be confidently asserted that this string of small islands stretching between Japan and Taiwan is a birthplace of some of the finest weaving in the world. One cannot help wondering how people could have been blind to this fact for so long. The climate nourishes indigo in the hills and yellow on the flatlands and even the *beni* flower from which the lovely bright red is made. And as for materials for weaving, there is banana fibre in plenty. From the richness of such gifts of nature this birth of craft took place.

POTTERY

Japan is a land of potters. Smoke rises from kilns all over the country. Potters are numerous, and their pots innumerable. Unfortunately the innate beauty of their work has suddenly deteriorated. The techniques and materials and men remain, but good pots are vanishing. Shape and pattern have become false. It seems that good ware for everyday use, as in the past, can no longer be produced. A small amount of unspoiled stoneware made for local use remains, such as that of Naeshirogawa. But life has altered and the local demand has vanished, so that even in these last strongholds one cannot say how long the local traditions will last.

As I see it, during the last half century the capacity to see and value what is good and true has been lost under the impact of industrialism. As long as tradition lasted all was well, but now, with new forms of living and with new methods having replaced the old group handwork—and without the selective power of the individual to replace tradition—there appears to be no answer to the problem. Hitherto such a devolution had never occurred in Japan. It seems that nothing but bad work results, for even among the artist, or individual, craftsmen, few produce work at all comparable with that guided by tradition.

In this situation the only pottery to which I can point with approval is that of Tsuboya of the Ryūkyūs (Plates 51–54). I think their pots are best in all Japan today, but have been unnoticed hitherto. These kilns are remote and were probably considered small and insignificant, but their history of three hundred years is comparable with that of Naeshirogawa (Plates 55, 56). During this time a great variety of pots have been made there; in fact, few potteries, if any, have produced such varied techniques from such few kilns. Perhaps due to many different influences, one can find almost all the main techniques represented in the Tsuboya pots. Their overglaze enamels on stoneware and their sgraffito patterns through white slip are particularly noteworthy. The famous old Japanese Inuyama enamelled stoneware does not attain this quality. The Tsuboya pieces have a warmth of feeling only comparable with Chinese Sung dynasty enamelled stoneware. It is the quality of the white slip and the manner of its use that is responsible for this. Also, the use of the engraved line through this white slip is unlike that of other potteries. Over the engraving cobalt blue and amber glazes are dabbed or washed, producing effects not to be found elsewhere. In comparison with other kilns, the liveliness of pattern has been retained. The same thing is also true of the vitality of the shapes. And yet even at Tsuboya one looks ahead with apprehension, because the potters do not really understand the value of what they make and are defenceless against the encroachments of the machine age.

Besides glazed wares, Tsuboya still produces quantities of unglazed stoneware jars of large size for the storage of the Okinawan spirits called *awamori*. The forms are splendid, and the workmanship without fault. Some potters tried imitating these shapes, but the results were too artful. Such austere unglazed jars were much appreciated by men of Tea, but their taste had become ritualistic and congealed, whereas the Okinawan potters remain free, unconscious, and powerful.

These qualities spring from their way of life and its honesty and naturalness. For that reason I decry the patronizing attitude with which they have been hitherto regarded. They do not employ machinery to increase output, but they have a natural power absent in modern factories. Time means little to them, and this timelessness releases this natural power. I want to tell everyone that this naturalness ought to be valued and nursed, for it is life itself.

The potteries themselves, too, form a harmonious whole with the village, which can scarcely be found anywhere. Roads wind between clay walls, like those of Korean villages. The dark green leaves of overhanging flowering trees against the red-and-white tiled roofs are beautiful.

I have described only a few of the treasures of Okinawa, but there are so many others: food, without the taste of which one hardly enters into the life of these people; their stone roads and paths, which put so many Japanese gardens to shame; the grotesque free sculptures on the rooftops; the lacquer utensils and furnishings; the cut of their garments; the turn of their phrases; their rites and legends—all of which I would like to dwell upon. I have said so little, but if my lame words ring any bells in the minds of my readers I shall be thankful for the sake of the future of these people and their rope of islands.

1939

Hakeme

In order to give dark clays a white effect, liquid coatings of white clay may be applied to them. The one of which I shall write is the application with a very coarse brush of thick white engobe, or slip, to the raw body, which was so admirably used by Korean potters.

If there were an abundance of white clay suitable for the body of the pots, there would be no need for coating. In practise, though, such white clay is scarce, while brown clay is found in many places, so the latter is used and coated with the former. This is due partly, no doubt, to the widespread human desire for whiteness and purity, but also to a desire to make profitable use of white clay not otherwise usable. Interestingly enough, it frequently happens that where the white clay of the slip and the brown body clay come from the same area, they go well together.

In the East a plain coating is enjoyed, but a Western public appears to be unsatisfied with this restraint and demands further decoration. There are two methods of coating a dark clay body: dipping the pots in white slip, and brushing on the slip. The former is the simplest and commonest method, but if the properties of the body and slip are not well matched, the slip tends to flake off the fired piece, and also this process often damages the body surface. The brushing method probably developed to counteract this tendency, since the slip takes to the surface better. Another, and perhaps more urgent, reason was to economize on white slip when it had run out or was difficult to obtain, since the coarse brushing used far less clay. In this sense, roughly brushed slip developed as a simplification of the regular dipping method, and as such was often used for cheap, coarse vessels.

171

There is also a variant of this method in which the thick slip is applied by a series of rhythmic taps with a large, round, soft brush somewhat like a dish mop. The usual slip brush in both cases is made of hair, hemp fibre, tail ends of rice straw, or grasses. Even a cotton rag is used. With such simple tools the slip is applied swiftly and broadly. The result is variegated and shows the scrape of the fibres. This is the effect that is called *hakeme* (literally, "brushmark"), something cheap and simple and for normal daily life (Plate 4).

It has no parallel in the West. One cannot help wondering why, but I think these may be the reasons. Western peoples seem to be repelled by roughness and more attracted by the finished, the smooth, and the regular. The development of Western science might be attributed to this same love of the precise. The Oriental, conversely, seeks the natural, the irregular, and the free, a tendency that finds natural expression in things such as *hakeme*. In short, where the Occidental sees only disharmony in *hakeme*, the Oriental sees harmony.

The Koreans are the masters of the irregular, and they invented the effects and loved *hakeme*. The finest white slip work is called *Mishima*, and in Japan it followed two clearly distinguishable courses. In one case, the brushing on of the white slip was dictated by necessity, as in Korea; examples are also found in crockery produced in Kyushu. But gradually, on the other hand, the beauty of *hakeme* came to be prized for its own sake, and the Japanese began consciously to attempt to produce beautiful *hakeme*. The result in this case was not crockery for everyday use but bowls for use in the Tea ceremony. In Korea, of course, no *hakeme* was ever made for such an artistic purpose; it was simply a technique dictated by practical necessity. The *hake-Mishima* Tea-bowls so prized by the Japanese Tea masters were originally not intended for the Tea ceremony, but for everyday use by poor peasants. It is significant, then, that where beauty is concerned, Japanese *hakeme*, produced by men with aesthetic awareness, cannot compare with the original Korean *hakeme*. Over and over again the Japanese have tried to reproduce the subtle effect of the original *hakeme*, but have never seen anything to match the originals. The beauty of Korean *hakeme*, one might almost say, is a kind of aesthetic *kōan*, the solution of which gives the key to the nature of beauty as such.

Of course, the talk here of *kōan* is the unhappy lot of us in our self-awareness; the Koreans concerned did their work in a state of mind blissfully innocent of the need, even, for such riddles. Indeed, far from considering their bowls as "beautiful", they almost certainly took a naïve pleasure in having achieved the desired effect by such simple means. It was a humble type of labour. They did not do it for its beauty, they merely did it. And yet, "merely doing" something is in itself a great source of beauty, implying as it does a state of freedom not bound by concepts of beauty, much less fear of the ugly. Questions such as the true nature of beauty were utterly remote from the Koreans of the day.

Interestingly enough, it was left to the Japanese to discover an unparalleled beauty in pottery born under such circumstances. In that sense, *hake-Mishima* found a true friend in the Japanese; without the Japanese eye for beauty, it might well have vanished into limbo along with the mass of other ordinary crockery.

Nevertheless, the Japanese achievement consisted solely in the discovery as such. When they tried to create on the basis of that discovery, they failed miserably. As a result, *Mishima* was to have no true progeny in Japan. Why should this paradox have arisen?

The reason is very plain: the beauty of Korean *hakeme* was created before there was any question of beauty, and to try to create it after that question has arisen is a contradiction in terms. The difference between something born of innocence and something created consciously is a difference between the safe and the perilous. The latter is created out of a swirling vortex of beauty and ugliness. That is why the *hakeme* attempted by the Japanese potters carries no guarantee of security, whereas the Korean *hakeme* is created in the security of a realm where ugliness has no place, a realm where the interference of conceptualization cannot exist from the outset, much less the trouble of getting rid of it. Its beauty is not beauty as the antithesis of ugliness. Japanese *hakeme*, on the other hand, has the eternal weakness that, being concerned above all with the pursuit of beauty, it is fated to remain captive to that idea.

The beauty of Korean *hakeme* is inexhaustible; one may look at it indefinitely without tiring, and it is no wonder that the Tea masters with their keen perception of beauty were instantly captivated by it. What is the nature of that beauty? One may sense in it the essential rhythms of human life, in their most unadorned form, appearing in constantly undulating curves. They are the spontaneous pulsations of life, recalling the natural rhythms of the winds that blow, the streams that flow, and the clouds that rise into the air. They could be called a direct manifestation of the natural life lived by those who made the pots, of the placid frame of

173

mind in which they rose and lay down in harmony with nature. Compared with theirs, how unnatural are our lives today, how they fly in the face of nature. True humanity and naturalness have become distressingly remote from our existence.

Since a brush is used for *hakeme*, it naturally leaves a number of more or less parallel lines. At the same time, since the movement of the brush is not calculated, the lines have a freedom that truly parallel lines could not have. They are regular yet not regular, irregular yet not irregular, in a subtle way that no deliberate effort could achieve—the kind of wondrous effect only attainable by someone in a state of "non-conceptualization".

Japanese *hakeme*, in its pursuit of beauty, is a process of artificial creation based from start to finish on conscious ideas. For this reason Japanese *hakeme*, being inspired by the moving mind, has none of that stillness in movement that characterizes the Korean original. The Korean pieces are the results of trusting everything to the materials and tools, the maker remaining hidden. There was no idea of creating a beauty full of spontaneous energy—and it is precisely here that lies the mysterious source of its free and untrammelled vigour.

The *hake-Mishima* Tea-bowls, moreover, were the everyday ware of the time, being produced rapidly and in great numbers. This rapid process of endless repetition is, in itself, inducive of forgetfulness of the self, of the transcending of the self, and of a state, eventually, where the work "does itself". How unthinkable that a potter should ever have signed his name on a piece of Korean *hakeme*! How different they are from the Japanese pots on each of which is carefully inscribed the maker's name! It is the humble on whom heaven's grace falls in full measure. In this sense, *hake-Mishima* is a typical example of work that depends on grace.

However, if someone else, startled by its beauty, tries to create that beauty for himself, he will find himself obliged to depend not on grace but on conscious effort. He must rely on his own skill in making it. How different the two pictures this suggests: the peasant quietly repeating the process of production; and the potter struggling to give birth to a work of art. This is not to say that the results of the latter are without worth, but the way is perilous, and the work produced tends to become too self-assertive. The marks of the brush strive so hard after freedom that they become constrained in the effort. This, it would seem, is why the resulting *hakeme* is never anything but unnatural. It is difficult to transcend the self through conscious effort. The man of great spiritual experience may occasionally achieve naturalness; but by then he will probably have experienced for himself the essential ordinariness of *hakeme*, have reached that instant where conscious effort at last comes into contact with grace. The Tea masters' greatest oversight was that they perceived the *hakeme*'s beauty, but not the grace that glowed within it; if they had done so, they would not have placed such overweening trust in themselves.

Some inkling of the truth, perhaps, led them to try asking Zen monks to make *hakeme*. A priest who had achieved Enlightenment, they reasoned, should be able to wield the brush unhindered by intellectual preoccupations. Here, the Japanese must be credited with considerable fineness of insight. A thoroughly enlightened man might indeed be able to achieve a free line of a kind. Yet depth of faith or philosophy is not enough in the crafts. The materials, tools, and techniques will not grant one freedom at once. One should not, in such a case, consider that the freedom exists in the human being; one should seek freedom, rather, in the work that emerges spontaneously when one entrusts oneself to the materials and the tools.

The same, inevitable process is to be seen in all true craft work. It is not accidental, yet neither is it artificial. It is governed by the same kind of laws that make water run downhill and clouds rise. A Zen monk, since he is presumably well aware of such things, should surely become conscious of his own handicap when confronted with the beauty of *hakeme*. The brush and the clay do not allow of dilettantism. Any amateur who takes up the brush will at once discover his own disability. Admittedly, so long as one is willing to accept that disability, a "natural" result of a kind may be achieved, just as in the paintings of children. But an adult will soon find that to let the brush have its own way is no easy matter. And when he realizes that, where *hakeme* is concerned, freedom comes from infinite repetition of a technique, he will feel ashamed of his attempt to create beauty in a few tries. In a sense, he will not be spiritually ready for the task until he has admitted humbly that it is beyond him.

As has been mentioned, this *hakeme* technique is Far Eastern, and the best examples have no added pattern. These are, even now, very little known in the West. When I showed projections of them abroad, however, the potters responded with warmth, and I expect most people, with eyes to see, would do so too, even if they look at them from a loophole in a world of very deliberately designed industrial products. It would seem that they are about to be influenced by that look, but I fear that they will make the same mistake that we have made. There is a great need to realize that this is a matter of full understanding and not just a new technique.

As to the technique employed: the slip is applied after the turning is finished and while the pot is still green hard. There are three procedures. First, brushing slip inside and out after scraping; secondly, with some clays, this may be done before scraping; thirdly, brushing slip inside the pot immediately after swabbing with water, if this suits the nature of the clay. Almost anybody finds these treatments lovely to watch. Salt, sugar, a seaweed glue, and even acid are added to some white clays to help them adhere. The softer the clay to which the slip is applied, the less likelihood of flaking taking place later. If the application is done on the throwing wheel, it is usually done when the wheel is in very slow motion.

Few methods of decorating pots are as free. I like those best that are left without added pattern, for in their flowing naturalness the imagination of the beholder is stirred to the greatest degree. The absence of painted pattern evokes the patterns of dreams; the looker becomes an artist; with the freedom of the brush he becomes free; he beholds the Kingdom of Beauty. They were Japanese eyes who first saw this province; my desire is that its beauty should delight the eyes of the world. Some Western potters have seen it already and carried its name, *hakeme*, abroad, but the meaning behind the word, which I have attempted to indicate, contains a challenge. The *hakeme* Tea-bowl is the objective challenge of Zen to them. What is their answer going to be?

This chapter was written by me (ten years ago) as part of a book, *The Book of Pots*, which I was hoping to publish. The outcome of long discussions between Bernard Leach, Shōji Hamada, Kanjirō Kawai, and myself, it was intended to cover the whole field of pottery. In its scope and in its search for meaning and standards it would have been of great value to others as well as ourselves, but sickness and the return of Leach to England prevented me from making more than rough outline of the discussion that took place and from finishing more than a quarter of that book.

1954

The Way of Tea

THEY SAW; BEFORE ALL ELSE, they saw. They were able to see. Ancient mysteries flew from this well-spring of seeing.

Everyone looks at things, but people do not perceive in the same manner. Some are able to penetrate into the depths of things, but most see only the surface, and objects are usually categorized as right or wrong. To misapprehend is no better than not to notice. Though everyone says he sees things, how few can see things as they are. Among these few are found the early masters of the Way of Tea. They had deep-seeing eyes. They could comprehend intuitively. And with this penetration, they saw truth.

What was their way of seeing? They saw directly. Most people look through some medium, generally interposing thoughts, personal tastes, and habits between the eye and the object. Assuredly, the result is different points of view; but it is quite another thing to see directly. Seeing directly constitutes a direct communion between the eye and the object. Unless a thing is seen without mediation, the thing itself cannot be grasped. Only the men who possess this capacity of direct perception are true masters of Tea, just as those who can see God with immediacy are the real priests worthy of the name. True men of Tea are masters of the power of seeing.

What, then, did the Tea masters see—what did their vision disclose? It was the reflection of the inner nature of things, the reality of things, which the old philosophers called "the eternal mode". They saw the thing itself, the whole, which is entirely different from the sum total of the parts. The whole is indivisible; it cannot be divided. To see the whole directly means to see before thinking, without time for analysis or discrimination. If we look at things with our thoughts, we see only a portion, and if we use intellect before we see, understanding is superficial. More can be learned through the power of seeing the whole directly than through intellection. There is a passage in a religious book that reads: "He who would know before he believeth cometh never to the true knowledge of God". It is the same with the beautiful. Those who employ intellect before they see are denied a real comprehension of beauty. Before all else, old masters of Tea saw.

If the eye is clear, it functions promptly. As it penetrates, it is free of doubt. Doubt begets thought; thought bedims the eye. To see full in the face is to see clearly. If we see clearly, there is no time to hesitate. Thus, seeing is at once believing. We believe because we can see clearly; the revelation of the reality of the thing induces belief. Those who see directly are quick in their apprehension. The working of the eye transcends time. Discernment of the good from the bad is instantaneous. People free of doubt are bold. The seers, therefore, made discoveries; diverse things were born of the Tea masters' eyes.

With these men, seeing was identical with creating. All the *ō-meibutsu* ("great masterpieces" of Tea utensils), no matter by whom or where or when they were originally produced, may well be said to have been the creations of the eminent Tea masters, for their perception created things freely and without reserve.

The founders of the Way of Tea did not see things by means of convention; rather, it was their vision that brought the rules and conventions into being. How widely they differ in this respect from the later devotees of Tea! Tea that has degenerated into mannerism is not Tea. When things are not seen directly, Tea loses its fundamentals. Tea always teaches the necessity of going straight to the object. It does not teach us to look at things through Teaism. If we are enslaved by Tea, we lose sight of its truth. Unless we purify our eyes, how can we keep Tea pure?

But seeing was not the sole merit of the Tea masters. They did not stop there, for merely to see is not seeing completely. Seeing led them to using, and using led to seeing still deeper. Without using there is no complete seeing, for nothing so emphasizes the beauty of things as their right application. Through use, therefore, the Tea masters approached still closer to the secrets of beauty. If we want to see a thing well, we must use it well. Not only did the Tea masters enjoy beauty with the eye and contemplate it with the mind, but they also experienced it with the whole being. We might say they comprehended beauty in action. Tea is not mere passive appreciation of beauty. To live beauty in our daily lives is the genuine Way of Tea.

The Way of Tea is the mode of looking at utensils and the code of conduct of handling them. Everyone uses utensils daily, but distinctions arise involving what utensils are used, and still greater ones arise involving how they are used. That is, everyone may use utensils, but the things used are various and the ways they are handled are different. Some do not use what they should; others use what they should not. Some do not care what they use; others do not trouble themselves about the way they use what they use. Can such people be rightly called users?

The manner of choice is decisive, and the manner of use enlivens or kills. Misuse is worse than non-use, yet there are more ways than one to use things. The changings of the seasons, the alternation of morning and evening, the very rooms, the personalities of articles themselves—all these call for an endless creativeness. Utensils have to wait for men just as men wait for them. It may be easy to use things, but how many know how to use them? True men of Tea adapted things into their most intimate lives and mastered them. From seeing things they went on to using them. That they lived beauty in their practical life is truly their greatest service.

But what did they use? It was not that they used merely what was available. They chose things that had heretofore not been so used. It is even probable they did not always know for what use some utensils had been intended. It was the objects' beauty that made the men of Tea wish to adapt them to their own daily lives. They invented methods of application, thus making the things useable. In the end they went so far as to think that nothing else could be utilized; they thought that no other articles for such use existed. Today everyone regards these utensils as things created for the use of Tea. The Tea masters created these utensils and originated their uses. Apart from this creation, the Way of Tea would not have existed. It was not that Tea utensils existed previously for men of Tea to use, but that they used to the greatest advantage the things that they thought beautiful. Thus, the objects they mastered became Tea utensils. Things that cannot be used possess something negative, even if beautiful. Ugly things are not fit to be used. Real beauty appeals to us, asks to be used; beauty cannot be neglected. The seeing eye will urge the using hand.

In this manner was the Way of Tea born. Instead of the utensils being its result, they created it. The seeing eye and the using hand made Tea utensils from ordinary objects. When there are no beautiful utensils, there is no real Tea; without the power to create beautiful utensils, there can be no Tea. Some say Tea independent of utensils is possible, others complain that because they have no proper Tea utensils they cannot enjoy Tea. Both speak but small truth. Without the eye that can discern suitable utensils, how can Tea be preserved? And without the power to create such utensils, how can Tea flourish? Granting, even that there are utensils, if we cannot use them properly, of what does Tea consist?

The remarkable accomplishment of the great Japanese men of Tea is that they started a new development in the making of utensils. Common wares were transformed into Tea utensils because the masters saw and used them. No such Tea utensils existed before; they came into being only through the masters. What then, of the utensils that were created after them? What, for instance, of the later *chūkō-meibutsu* (masterpieces of the revival), which are counted among the treasured utensils? How inferior when compared with the old *ō-meibutsu*! Should we not be ashamed to show them to the great masters of past centuries? Indeed, the authentic beauty of the *ō-meibutsu* is sublime.

But it must be remembered that these enduring "great masterpieces" were originally but ordinary, neglected wares. Only the coming of the Tea masters ennobled them into exquisite Tea utensils. And through the seeing eye, we, too, are able to increase the number of *ō-meibutsu*. The world is full of hidden beauty, and only a limited portion of it was discovered by the great masters. There must be countless masterpieces waiting for us to bring them to light. At present there are no masters who can use these unfortunate utensils perfectly and thus exalt them to *ō-meibutsu*. The appearance of such modern genius would infinitely enhance the glory of the founders of the Way of Tea.

How, then, did the Tea masters use these objects? Magnificently! They were neither merely ingenious in application nor simply concerned with practicality.

The modes practised by the Tea masters passed into laws. In time, it came to be felt that the only correct use was that prescribed by the masters. Who else could employ the utensils with the same profound insight? However, not to them alone did the modes they invented belong. They were elevated into a form, and that form transcended the individual,

180

even the Tea master. It became a universal law. How the methods of the masters became law is indeed extraordinary.

This does not mean that the masters thought out the forms beforehand and then adapted them to the social custom of drinking a certain hot beverage. Use the right utensils in the right place at the right time, and you will find that it coincides with the law. The most efficient use—that, in itself, assumes a definite form. This form is the crystallization of the manner of use. Boil a thing down and you will get its essence. That is the form, the Way. Unless an article is used to this extent, its use is not complete. If the extent of use is incomplete, the article is not really used; when it is really used, we shall find it used according to the law. The form of Tea is a necessity, not a device. Can there be anything more natural than the law?

Tea is, therefore, the Way. Since it is the Way, it is universal. It is a law to which one naturally conforms. Tea does not admit personal likes and dislikes. It is not such a shallow thing as to trifle with individual tastes. The Way of Tea transcends the individual. Its law is the beauty of Tea. Tea that expresses individuality cannot be the right Tea. It must belong to all. It is not a private path, but a highway for humanity.

Thus Tea has been referred to as a ceremony. A ceremony presupposes ritual pattern. Having universality and having become ritual, it can now claim a name, the Way of Tea. This Way claims our service. The ritual of Tea has invested it with authority, and its disciples must be loyal and obedient to the ritual. Some may regard obedience as a restraint, but to obey a law is to conform to it, and that is absolute liberty. Liberty must not be confused with wilfulness. Perfect freedom lies only in observing the law. Wilfulness is the heaviest of fetters; self-assertion binds us hand and foot. Ceremonial Tea is the road to freedom. Here, and here only, can be found the profound significance of all the traditional arts. In what other forms can we find both the beauty of the Nō drama and the art of the Kabuki theatre? Every new thing is admittedly destined to stabilization in its own form, which in the course of its development it will naturally acquire. Tea attains its consumate beauty in its forms. Tea devotees must respect the law. The longevity of Tea depends solely on the existence of these forms. Tea ceremony continues forever, unaffected by the death of the founder or the coming and going of successive masters. It is super-human; time cannot efface it. Many a false Tea master may succeed, yet Tea as a form will remain unchanged. If it had not been raised to a ritual, its history might long since have run its course. A thing limited to individuals is but short lived.

Surviving to this day are not the persons but the forms. Yet, oh for real Tea masters who could inspire the forms! The forms at present have paled to a shadow. It is deplorable that there are so many who misapprehend and distort them. They adhere too strictly to the forms and fail to grasp the spirit. No one hurts Tea more seriously than he who mistakes these essential forms for superficial patterns. The two must be clearly distinguished. The Tea that exaggerates the importance of the outward forms only is offensive.

Tea is often severely criticized as an art of formalities. But this is a misconception. It is the fault of man, not of Tea, that the soul of the forms has been destroyed. What can be more alive and vigorous than the law? How many have killed Tea by misapprehending the profound significance of the rite! How long has the true spirit of the forms been fading! If in conforming with the rite we feel fettered, we have not yet mastered it. We had better not trifle with Tea in its outer forms. We must not make light of them. When the forms are complete, Tea is a living thing. Real Tea is free and flexible in its forms. The greatest achievement of the arts is the discovery of law. Tea is one Way to discover the law of beauty.

It was the Tea masters themselves who truly loved things, and because of them the things were endowed with value. But they did not claim that the right to love things was exclusively theirs. The objects they cared for are worthy of love by any person at any time, any place. The masters were not partial in their choosing, nor was their choice eccentric or peculiar. They never looked at things subjectively, but received them just as they were. Naturally, the objects they loved are worthy of universal love.

True lovers cannot but share their love with others. These utensils, because they were so greatly loved, call out, "Look at us!" They will not be out-rivalled by any famous art masterpiece.

Those who have eyes to see cannot help but entertain a warm affection for the masters who discovered this beauty. Kindred spirits commune with each other. In the Tea utensils, the masters chose for all people. They established a communal focus. If we cannot perceive, the fault lies with us and not with the utensils, much less with the masters. All people invariably love what the masters loved because they loved objectively and not subjectively. Their love embraced the love of all mankind. If we find anything truly lovable, we love it in the same way as they did.

Therefore, we must feel that the things they loved were the most lovable things. If beautiful things are found that they did not discover, such things will be seen to have the same qualities as those they loved. The objects of their love stand for all things lovable. When our love for things deepens, we shall be aware that we turn to the beauty they loved. Should we happen to meet a thing of excellent quality, we long more to show it to the masters who are gone than to anyone else. When we speak about the beautiful, we are in fact speaking about them. It can even be said that all beautiful things are ever being seen as if by them; and all eyes are embraced in theirs.

It follows that the things they loved are what all people wish to love. So it is with the Tea utensils. Through them the Tea masters expressed the universal aspects of beauty.

Thus, the Tea masters made an extraordinary achievement; in the utensils they selected, they presented us with the final criterion of ideal beauty. Tea has faithfully fulfilled its part in diffusing this gift. The people were given a simple rule with which to measure the mystery called beauty. Can one offer a more wonderful gift? It was given to all, to the world, and is an infallible standard that no one can possibly misuse. The votaries of Tea were not its sole beneficiaries; it is serviceable to all people, just as is a foot-rule, to measure quite plainly and easily the degree of inexplicable beauty.

That it is not at all complicated is the greatest wonder. It is the simplest rule in the world. How does it measure? In a single epithet: by the word *shibui*. Nothing else whatever. This is quite enough to make it function perfectly. The world may abound with different aspects of beauty. The lovely, the powerful, the gay, the smart—all belong to the beautiful. Each person, according to his disposition and environment, will feel a special affinity to one or another aspect. But when his taste grows more refined, he will necessarily arrive at the beauty that is *shibui*. Beauty cannot rest until it reaches this point. If one seeks depth in beauty, this stage must be attained some day. Many a term will serve to denote the secret of beauty, but this is the final word. Our Tea masters expressed their conception of consummate beauty with this word as standard.

It follows that all people must learn the use of this word in their judgement of the beautiful. With this as a criterion, we can see clearly the things in which the masters took delight. We can also understand their ways of seeing things. We poor mortals can, with the help of this fundamental word, measure the qualities of beauty. We shall therefore be sure to estimate correctly, no matter what the subject. *Shibui* is the sesame to open the doors to the infinite mysteries of beauty.

The Japanese are fortunate in that they comprehend this word. Of this precious adjective they make everyday use. Even the ignorant continually utter this word in their casual talk. They often go so far as to apply it to test the quality of their own taste. Even those who pursue the gay and gaudy are aware, deep down in their hearts, of the profundity of *shibui* beauty. This is the canon for beauty for all Japanese people. Do other peoples possess an equivalent? The lack of the word will mean the lack of the idea and fact. With the exception of this little Japanese word *shibui*, there is no such simple word, in the vocabulary of any nation, to indicate the criterion for the highest beauty. And that word is not expressed by difficult Chinese characters. Neither did the masters borrow an abstract word of the intellect. They employed a simple adjective, *shibui*, to describe a profound, unassuming, quiet feeling. Such a connotation was possible in the Orient alone, perhaps.

We also have the word *wabi*, bequeathed to us by Bashō, our greatest haiku poet. Though votaries of haiku poetry particularly realize its full significance, *wabi* is the objective for which we all strive—literati as well as laymen. But to expect its full comprehension by all people would be asking too much. For the idea cannot be demonstrated by physical sense; it must be conveyed by formless spirit. On the contrary, *shibui* is communicable by matter. It can be demonstrated in shape, in colour, and in pattern. In the Tea utensils, with their simplicity of shape, tranquillity of surface, mellow sombreness of colouring, chaste beauty of figure—in these living realities, the essence of the word can be captured, even by inferior intellects. That Tea masters have shown beauty in the shape of concrete things is their virtue and a fact that cannot be overlooked. *Shibusa* (the noun form) is not something distant, intangible, but a reality at hand. It invokes the abstract by means of the concrete. It is a mirror reflecting inner nature.

Wabi and *shibusa*, then, stand for one and the same thing. But whereas the word *wabi* belongs to the vocabulary of the select few, *shibusa* is overheard in the common parlance of the masses. How fortunate that there exists such a word, leading the people to an understanding of beauty! No, it leads the people to the *shibui* beauty, to ultimate beauty, to beauty consummate.

The chosen vessels are of the rarest quality. Something out of the common must lie hidden there, for we are never weary of admiring them. They are flawless treasures, possessing the so-called Ten Virtues of a masterpiece. Of that we may be assured.

If what the masters had marvelled at had been something merely unusual, they would have been nothing exceptional. Anyone could have done that. But the masters' eyes were more penetrating. They did not see the extraordinary in the extraordinary. Therein lies their merit. They did not draw their cherished treasures out of the valuable, the expensive, the luxurious, the elaborate or the exceptional. They selected them from the plain, the natural, the homely, the simple, and the normal. They explored the uneventful, normal world for the most unusual beauty. Can anything be more uncommon than to see the uncommon in the commonplace?

Most of us today have grown so commonplace that we cannot see the extraordinary save in the exceptional. The early Tea masters apprehended the profundity of normal things. Out of unregarded ordinary articles they selected the exquisite Tea things. Is it not incredible that the Tea-bowls and Tea-caddies, now ranked as ō-meibutsu ("great masterpieces"), were once the commonest of wares?

Truth always nestles close to us. The Tea masters cast their caressing eyes upon their surroundings. Their vision encompassed articles of everyday use, the things everybody ignores. We might say that the Tea masters had great boldness. Yet nothing was more natural. Even the common articles made for daily use become endowed with beauty when they are loved. The humble are receptive to love. These articles were born pure in heart and were nurtured with nature's blessing. They are sound both in mind and substance. If they had been too delicate, or too showy, they could not have served as utensils. Is not sincerity their primary virtue? It is no wonder they radiate true beauty. To such is the kingdom of heaven promised; the humble are closely related to beauty. These masterpieces were once humble household utensils. Their beauty shines forth from their natural simplicity. Those articles that lack the noble quality of humility cannot be made into good Tea things.

Let us now put the matter this way. Did the Tea masters choose those beautiful utensils from the merely decorative, from art for art's sake? By no means! Utensils meant for practical life were their best and constant friends. It was not lofty, unapproachable beauty, but beauty interwoven with the actualities of life that the Tea masters found. They formed stronger attachment for visible beauty than for ideological beauty. They sought beauty not in the brain but in life itself. They drew beauty to them, so to speak, and made it their familiar. They perceived the essence of beauty in intimacy. Thus they combined beauty and life. Is it possible to find a more impressive example in the history of aesthetic appreciation?

Naturally, that which strongly attracted their hearts corresponds with what today we call the arts of utility. They found a profounder beauty in the practical art born to answer the immediate needs of life than in the fine arts born for beauty's sake alone. They did not seek beauty apart from actual living. They found the highest and noblest aspects of beauty in the articles close to life. This was their insight and inner experience. To them the beautiful and the craftsmanlike were synonymous. They make a striking contrast to the aesthetes in our time who set value upon the merely artistic and scorn craftsmanship. Aesthetes try to appreciate beauty through ideas. Tea would not have come into being had this been its case.

Everything that concerns Tea, to say nothing of the utensils in particular, is related in one way or another to craftsmanship. In the hanging scrolls, for instance, we consider first their harmony with the mounting. Unless they show a craft value, they are never used. The Tea-room is a synthesis of craftsmanship. The Tea-garden is a craft adjustment of nature. The whole process of preparing and serving tea is nothing more than a craft movement of life. Each item has a beauty germinated in utility and rooted deep in real life. Tea is the patterning of the practical life, patterning in aesthetic dimensions. Isolated from craftsmanship, Tea cannot maintain its way. To apprehend beauty in crafts and crafts in beauty— that is the characteristic of Tea. Who else could exhort this with more conviction than the Tea masters? They never spoke of beauty except in connection with actual life. In this way they have conferred everlasting beauty upon the practical arts. The Way of Tea is the aestheticism of craftsmanship.

Tea, however, does not end with seeing, nor with using, and still less with its forms. To be sure, these are important elements. But it goes still deeper. Unless it leads to the Ultimate, it is not a Way. But since it is the Way, it cannot be superficial. Many patronize Tea, yet few indeed are admitted to the sanctuary of Tea; the Way is beyond superficial reach. Not everyone can practise Tea with full comprehension. When practised by a novice, it is apt to become a mere plaything, or at most, a pastime. When we make a little progress, we are captivated by our own cleverness, but the Way will have nothing to do with self-conceit, affection, fancifulness, or artifice. In this present age there is still an apparent enthusiasm for Tea; but we cannot say that the Way itself is thriving. If we look back, we cannot but regret its present decline: we shall be struck with the realization that there is not even one real man of Tea living. The Way requires the profundity of the inner consciousness. Imperfection of skill, inferiority in the vessels, are of far less importance; if not mentally prepared, we fall little short of committing an overwhelming error. Without the proper depth of mind, Tea is not Tea.

Harmony, reverence, purity, and serenity are the inculcated traditional principles of Tea. But these demand spiritual preparation. It is no child's play. How can it be achieved without long, concentrated effort and endeavour? The Way leads us to greater heights—from the teaching of things to that of the spirit. Things are dead unless the mind animates them. We must strive until the possession of noble things becomes one with the possession of the noble mind. Unless a thing attracts the mind it is not a thing; unless the mind gives life to things it is not as yet complete. Many a beautiful thing may exist, but it cannot of itself become a utensil. It must first be the manifestation of the mind. Without the active mind, how can objects have life? Unless the mind is sincere, the objects themselves cannot be sincere. Matter and spirit are one in the process of Enlightenment. But though many provide themselves with things, very few endeavour to cultivate their minds. All those who clothe themselves in priestly robes are not worthy to be called monks; true monks only deserve to wear such robes. Many speak of Tea. But how many can be Tea monks?

Tea is a religion of beauty. It can claim to be called the Way of Tea only when it is exalted to a religion. Until the mind is ready, we cannot hope to enter the sanctuary of Tea. Is it not in order to prepare the mind that we handle the Tea utensils? Unless we have associated with things so intimately that we have purified our minds through them, it cannot be said that we really see things or use them. Merely to toy with things is to defile them; to defile them is to commit a sacrilege of the spirit. We may say that if the heart is stained we cannot enjoy divine intercourse with things. Until a utensil meets a sincere man, it cannot be called a worthy utensil.

The sanctuary of Tea is the sanctuary of the laws of beauty. The various sacred rules there current are comparable with those of a religion. Beauty and Faith are after all but phases of Truth. Tea and Zen have been closely connected since early times, as is most natural. Studying Zen through the intermediary of things is Tea. A Tea-bowl, as well as a flower vase, make the best themes for Zen meditation. Is there any difference between the contemplation of the arrangement of a tree or a stone in the Tea-garden and that of the meaning of a line or a passage of the sacred writings?

The quiet, simple Tea-room, too, corresponds with the silent meditation hall in a Zen monastery. Are the various Tea rituals also different from the regulations for the daily life of the monks? To realize beauty and to practise belief are one and the same thing. Such sayings as "To be is to be Buddha" and "Matter and spirit, one and the same" mean that the revelation of beauty and the revelation of Buddha are identical in their solemnity, warmth, purity, and peacefulness, and a Tea master and a Zen monk are two in body, but one in spirit, differing only in appearance. To study beauty in Tea is to face the direction of Absolute Enlightenment. If we want to realize in ourselves the Communion of Love and Reverence and practise Cleanliness and Sincerity, we must be immaculate in spirit. Tea is, after all, a way of self-discipline. To the self-conceited, the haughty, the luxurious, the impure, the affected—to all these the sacred gate of beauty is inaccessible. How numerous are those who covet things, and how few are those who devote themselves to the enlightenment of their spirits. But without the latter it is impossible to practise Tea. The Way of Tea is indubitably a self-disciplinary way.

This teaching is already four centuries old. But what has age to do with its essence? It is, like Zen, ever fresh and vigorous in spite of its antiquity. There must lie latent some incorruptible vitality that has permitted it to continue to attract generation after generation. Some believe it to be a mere formality of the past. But if the rituals are stagnant, it is because of misapplication, not because of the Tea ceremony itself.

Old though the doctrines of Confucius and Mencius are, the moral law will always go back to them, a well ever fresh if only people will draw from it. In like sense, the guilt of killing the spirit of Tea in its outer forms is to be laid to would-be masters, and not to those free from the influence of both people and time.

Man may discard Tea, but he cannot do away with the law of Tea. The Way of Tea is the law of beauty. If a new form of beauty comes into being, Tea also will find a new form. Even if there be two forms of beauty, old and new, there can be no priority and posterity to the laws of beauty. Tea is not a kind of beauty, but the law of beauty.

All who wish to study and live beauty in their lives must be at home in the principles of Tea. Seeking after beauty and Tea are the same thing. It cannot be otherwise.

The aesthetic sensibility and culture of the Japanese may be attributed to the discipline of Tea through many years. But at present, when the power of seeing beauty has so sadly fallen away, the mission of the Tea ceremony appears still greater. Above all else, anyone who intends to establish the Kingdom of Beauty here on earth cannot help reflecting upon the magnificent achievements of the Tea masters. We deem it our mission to prove ourselves their legitimate successors, thereby to revive the true spirit of Tea.

[I know of one experimental Tea ceremony at which Yanagi presided. There may have been other occasions but I feel certain that Yanagi did not establish his own ceremony. I spoke about the matter with him and felt that rather than attempting a premature form he preferred waiting for adjustment of cultures to take place naturally. He always laid stress upon the early Tea masters prior to Sen no Rikyū (1521–1591) and deplored the decay of the sumptuous Genroku era (1688–1704). With regard to ritual I am certain that Yanagi would have avoided extravagance and all mere formalism whilst always on the watch for significant beauty, both old and new. The utensils employed would have conformed to that noble simplicity contained in the adjective *shibui*.—B.L.]

1952

The Kizaemon Tea-bowl

THIS SINGLE TEA-BOWL IS CONSIDERED to be the finest in the world. There are three main kinds of Tea-bowls, those originating in China, Korea, and Japan, respectively. The most lovely are from Korea, and men of Tea always give them first place. Of these, there are many varieties, such as *Ido, Unkaku, Komogai, Goki, Totoya*, etc. The one considered most aesthetically satisfying is the *Ō Ido* ("Great" *Ido*). Again, there are varieties of *Ō Ido: Ko Ido, Ao Ido, Ido Waki*. The finest are called *meibutsu Ō Ido, meibutsu* signifying the particularly fine pieces. There are twenty-six bowls registered as *meibutsu*, but the finest of them all, and the one of which I shall write here, is that known as Kizaemon *Ido* (Plate 1). This bowl is said to contain the essence of Tea.

It is not known whence the word *Ido* derives; it was the name of the place where these pots came from in all probability. Kizaemon is a man's name—Takeda Kizaemon, a merchant of Osaka, who owned the bowl. A *meibutsu* has to have a pedigree [like an English racehorse]. Honda Tadayoshi, lord of Noto, possessed this bowl at the beginning of the seventeenth century. In 1634 it passed into the hands of Nakamura Sosetsu, a Tea master of Sakai. In 1751 it went to Toshi Ieshige, then in 1775, approximately, it became the property of Lord Matsudaira Fumai of Matsue, who was a great collector of Tea-bowls, at a price of 550 *ryō* (an immense sum). Fumai was exceedingly fond of it and kept it by him constantly. In 1818 he gave it to his son Gettan with the injunction, "This is one of the finest pieces in the land; you must treasure it always".

But this Tea-bowl got the reputation of bringing sickness and death to its owner. There was once a dilettante who owned this particular bowl.

He came down in the world and finally ended up as a groom for visitors to the Shimabara gay quarters in Kyoto, but he clung to the bowl without selling it. And the unhappy man was stricken with boils and died. From this time legend had it that a curse was associated with the bowl. It had this repute before Lord Matsudaira bought it, and he himself twice fell ill with a plague of boils. His wife begged him to get rid of it, but he refused, and his son Gettan inherited it in due course. Thereupon Gettan got a plague of boils, and the family gave it into the keeping of their priests in the Kohō-an, a subsidiary establishment of the Daitoku-ji temple in Kyoto, the site of the family graves. One can still see, hung up at the entrance to the temple, the palanquin that is said to have been used to bring the bowl in 1804. Before the Meiji era nobody could see it without the permission of the Matsudaira family. It is one hundred years since Matsudaira died; men die, but the bowl is as it always was.

In 1931 I was shown this bowl in company with my friend, the potter Kanjirō Kawai. For a long time I had wished to see this Kizaemon bowl. I had expected to see that "essence of Tea", the seeing eye of Tea masters, and to test my own perception; for it is the embodiment in miniature of beauty, of the love of beauty, of the philosophy of beauty, and of the relationship of beauty and life. It was within box after box, five deep, buried in wool and wrapped in purple silk.

When I saw it, my heart fell. A good Tea-bowl, yes, but how ordinary! So simple, no more ordinary thing could be imagined. There is not a trace of ornament, not a trace of calculation. It is just a Korean food bowl, a bowl, moreover, that a poor man would use every day—commonest crockery.

A typical thing for his use; costing next to nothing; made by a poor man; an article without the flavour of personality; used carelessly by its owner; bought without pride; something anyone could have bought anywhere and everywhere. That is the nature of this bowl. The clay had been dug from the hill at the back of the house; the glaze was made with the ash from the hearth; the potter's wheel had been irregular. The shape revealed no particular thought: it was one of many. The work had been fast; the turning was rough, done with dirty hands; the throwing slipshod; the glaze had run over the foot. The throwing room had been dark. The thrower could not read. The kiln was a wretched affair; the firing careless. Sand had stuck to the pot, but nobody minded; no one invested the thing with any dreams. It is enough to make one give up working as a potter.

In Korea such work was left to the lowest. What they made was broken in kitchens, almost an expendable item. The people who did this were clumsy yokels, the rice they ate was not white, their dishes were not washed. If you travel you can find these conditions anywhere in the Korean countryside. This, and no more, was the truth about this, the most celebrated Tea-bowl in the land.

But that was as it should be. The plain and unagitated, the uncalculated, the harmless, the straightforward, the natural, the innocent, the humble, the modest: where does beauty lie if not in these qualities? The meek, the austere, the unornate—they are the natural characteristics that gain man's affection and respect.

More than anything else, this pot is healthy. Made for a purpose, made to do work. Sold to be used in everyday life. If it were fragile, it would not serve its purpose. By its very nature, it must be robust. Its healthiness is implicit in its function. Only a commonplace practicality can guarantee health in something made.

One should correctly say, perhaps, that there is no chance for it to fall sick; for it is a perfectly ordinary rice bowl used every day by the poor. It is not made with thought to display effects of detail, so there is not time for the disease of technical elaboration to creep in. It is not inspired by theories of beauty, so there is no occasion for it to be poisoned by over-awareness. There is nothing in it to justify inscribing it with the maker's name. No optimistic ideals gave it birth, so it cannot become the play-thing of sentimentality. It is not the product of nervous excitement, so it does not harbour the seeds of perversion. It was created with a very simple purpose, so it shuns the world of brilliance and colour. Why should such a perfectly ordinary bowl be so beautiful? The beauty is an inevitable outcome of that very ordinariness.

Those who like the unusual are immune to the ordinary, and if they are aware of it at all, they regard it as a negative virtue. They conceive active beauty as our duty. Yet the truth is odd. No Tea-bowl exceeds in Ido bowl in beauty.

All beautiful Tea-bowls are those obedient to nature. Natural things are healthy things. There are many kinds of art, but none better than this. Nature produces still more startling results than artifice. The most detailed human knowledge is puerile before the wisdom of nature. Why should beauty emerge from the world of the ordinary? The answer is, ultimately, because that world is natural. In Zen there is a saying that at the far end of the road lies effortless peace. What more can be desired? So, too, peaceful beauty. The beauty of the Kizaemon Ido bowl is that of strifeless peace, and it is fitting that it should rest in that chapel, the Kōho-an, for in that quiet place it offers its silent answer to the seeker.

From my heart I am thankful for those discriminating eyes of the men of Tea who chose their Tea-bowls. It was by an extraordinary honesty and depth of perception that they formed their standards. In the whole world I know of no parallel. In their appreciation lay an astonishing creativity. Emerging from a squalid kitchen, the Ido bowl took its seat on the highest throne of beauty. The Koreans laughed. That was to be expected, but both laughter and praise are right, for had they not laughed they would not have been the people who could have made such bowls, and if they had not continued to laugh they could not have gone on making them; and on the other hand if they had not been made as commonplace crocks the Tea masters would not have selected them. The Koreans made rice bowls; the Japanese masters made them into Tea-bowls.

The Tea masters liked the fine netting of crackle on Ido bowls for the warm, fresh friendliness it gives. They found a charm when the glaze skipped in firing, and when a "landscape" formed in the pattern of mended cracks. They enjoyed free, rough turning and felt that many pots are incomplete without it. They gave great attention to the cutting of a foot-ring, and delighted in natural runs and drips of congealed glaze. Then again they developed a high appreciation for the internal volume and curves of bowls; they looked to see how green tea settles into them. They were particular how the rims of bowls feel to the lips and how the endless ring is varied. They embraced the shape and kissed the thickness. And they knew what heart's ease there was in a gentle deformity. Finally, they worked out the conditions that made a bowl beautiful; for all beauty is inseparable from laws.

If Ido bowls had not been recognized in Japan, their beauty might not have been perceived in Korea or elsewhere. Japan became the native land of the Ido Tea-bowl. In the Gospel of Matthew, it says Jesus was born rather in Bethlehem than in Nazareth. In this statement there is truth.

So far I have looked at the character of the Ido Tea-bowls from the point of view of the users, the Tea masters. Now I would like to consider them from the potter's angle. By whose hands was that remarkable beauty produced, to be later discovered by the sharp eyes of men of Tea? Whence came that power?

It is impossible to believe that those Korean workmen possessed intellectual consciousness. It was precisely because they were not intellectuals that they were able to produce this natural beauty. The bowls were not products of conscious effort by the individual. The beauty in them springs from grace. Ido bowls were born, not made. Their beauty is a gift, an act of grace. The seven rules evolved by the masters of Tea were born by nature rather than made by man. They did not own the laws of beauty. Laws exist in a realm that transcends the self and ownership. Laws are the work of nature, not the product of human ingenuity.

It is nature that makes laws work. To observe them is appreciation. Neither is a matter of the maker's intellectual ingenuity. The artistic qualities inherent in a Tea-bowl belong to nature in their origins and to intuition in their perception. There is no objection to seeing seven "things to see" (i.e., points that constitute the aesthetic appeal) in the Ido bowls. But this should not lead one to believe that they were made for the sake of these seven points. Nor should one assume that so long as these seven points are all present the result will be a beautiful bowl; for the points are a gift of nature, and not the product of conscious artifice. Yet how often in Japanese Tea-bowls have people laboured under the obvious delusion that you could create beauty by artificially lining up these seven qualities.

The Tea masters assert that Korean bowls are the best. It is an honest admittance. Why, one asks, do they surpass Japanese bowls? And the answer is that Japanese potters strove to make good pots according to accepted canons, or rules. To confuse the two approaches to pots, that of the maker and that of the user, is quite wrong. Production was poisoned by appreciation. Japanese bowls bear the scars of awareness. Raku Chōjirō, Honami Kōetsu, and other individual potters all to a greater or lesser degree suffer from the same sickness. It is all very well to find irregularities of form in Ido bowls charming, but to make pots with deliberate distortions is to immediately lose that charm. If glazes skip during the firing of a pot, it is natural, it may be a blessing in disguise, but deliberately to cause it to do so with the misguided idea of following some Tea master's rules is quite another matter.

The foot-ring of an Ido bowl is exceptionally beautiful, but to set out to copy its spontaneous irregularities is fatal; the beauty vanishes. All these wilful sorts of deformation are to be found in Japanese pots above all others. It is our specialized kind of ugliness, all in the pursuit of misconceived beauty. There are few parallels anywhere in the world. It is ironical that the Japanese Tea masters, whose appreciation of beauty was more profound than anybody else's, should have perpetuated, and still be perpetuating, this evil. There is hardly one bowl stamped with the Raku seal that escapes ugliness. By contrast, every single Ido Tea-bowl escapes. The Kizaemon Ō Ido bowl is the antithesis of and challenge to Raku.

As I have said, the eyes that first recognized this content in the Ido bowls were astounding in their perceptivity. Whence came this insight? Was their sense of appreciation different from others? The answer is simple: they saw things directly, and things appeared directly to them. To "see directly" here refers to unclouded intuitive perception. These men did not rely on certificates of authenticity. They did not rely on inscribed names. They did not ask whose work it was. They did not follow the judgements of others. They did not love a piece because it was old. They just looked at it directly. There was nothing between the thing and their eyes; their eyes were unclouded. That was why they could make a judgement unswayed by irrelevancies. The thing went into them, and they went into the thing. There was a healthy give-and-take between the two sides. There was an exchange of love.

Indeed, the only reason why Tea can constitute a religion of beauty is that the intuitive perception of beauty forms its basis. Intuition is its bedrock, just as intuition is the bedrock of religion. If a thing cannot be seen directly there can be no Way of Tea, nor any Tea-bowl. What can we learn from this?

With direct vision the real things of Tea can be found even today. Many great *meibutsu* can appear before our eyes tomorrow because there are still many products of craft in the world today that come out of like circumstance and have the same heartbeat, the same workmanship as those Ido bowls. So many worship those bowls because of the name, Ō Ido, and are thereby blinded to unseen Ō Ido around them. In actuality we today have more opportunities of seeing, of finding crafts of this order than the old Tea masters had. Were they to be amongst us once more, their tears would fall with delight, and they would be collecting newly seen things of Tea and adapting them for a new Way of Tea for all people. Direct vision makes hearts and eyes busy.

[Upon my first reading of this paragraph I was surprised almost to protest, but then I reflected on Yanagi's own work in the sheer opening of his own and all our eyes to the beauty and normality surrounding Japan, Korea, and China, while the attention of all was centred upon new, industrial products, most of which were poorly designed and even vulgar, even if utilitarian. Since 1931, handcrafts have deteriorated all over the world, but this fact does not undermine the truth of his contention.—B.L.]

As I held the Kizaemon Ido bowl in my hands, many thoughts passed through my mind. I thought of all the things I had collected over the years for the folkcraft museum, and then of this one bowl. It seemed to be telling me to go on with the work I had undertaken. I was reconvinced that the road behind me and the road ahead were right roads. I shall go on pointing to the brethren of the Ido as I travel so that things of beauty and truth, even if but a few, shall adorn the world of tomorrow. I shall tell of true beauty, and I shall strive to find the way for such things to be made again. The Kizaemon Ido was returned, repacked in its many boxes. I recognized a number of *kōans* that demanded my solution. As I left the temple gate the wind blowing through the Zen forest appeared to be charging me to, "Speak, speak!"

1931

The Way of Craftsmanship

I HAVE BEEN WRITING for a long time about crafts, digging into almost virgin soil, and what I say may seem strange to unaccustomed ears, dubious, and difficult to accept because it is contrary to prevalent thought. I have continuously received a flow of doubting enquiries from friends and strangers alike, so I decided to gather my ideas together in the form of a series of questions and answers reviewing the bone structure of my arguments.

Q. *What are crafts?*
A. Things made to be used by people in daily life, such as clothes and furniture. Something different from fine arts, such as pictures made to look at.

Q. *What is the particular kind of beauty in crafts?*
A. Beauty that is identified with use. It is beauty born of use. Apart from use there is no beauty of craft. Therefore, things made that do not stand up to use or that ignore utility can barely be expected to contain this kind of beauty.

Q. *What is the meaning you attach to the word "use"?*
A. The word is not to be understood merely in its materialistic sense. The reason for this is that mind and matter must not be thought of as separate. Use therefore covers both. Such objects are to be looked at and touched with the responsive feeling of pleasure in use. If crafts are only judged from a utilitarian point of view, then pattern, for example, is uncalled for. But good pattern adds to the function of that utensil. It

becomes an indispensable part of use. On the other hand, however useful an artifact may be, if it causes in the mind a feeling of ugliness, it detracts from total service. The issue becomes clear in the province of food. Satisfying the demand of hunger is not the sole object of good cooking. We need good presentation and good flavours—that helps our appetite. Again, use that fulfils the mind alone is meaningless, like a wax replica of food. By use, then, I intend the indivisibility of mind and matter.

Q. *What is the special quality of beauty in crafts?*
A. The special quality of beauty in crafts is that it is a beauty of intimacy. Since the articles are to be lived with every day, this quality of intimacy is a natural requirement. Such beauty establishes a world of grace and feeling. It is significant that in speaking of craft objects, people use terms such as savour and style. The beauty of such objects is not so much of the noble, the huge, or the lofty as a beauty of the warm and familiar. Here one may detect a striking difference between the crafts and the arts. People hang their pictures high up on walls, but they place their objects for everyday use close to them and take them in their hands.

Q. *How many types of craft are there?*
A.   CRAFT

FOLKCRAFTS		ARTIST CRAFTS	
GUILD CRAFTS	INDUSTRIAL CRAFTS	ARISTOCRATIC CRAFTS	INDIVIDUAL CRAFTS

FOLKCRAFTS—unself-consciously handmade and unsigned for the people by the people, cheaply and in quantity, as for example, the Gothic crafts, the best work being done under the Medieval guild system.
INDIVIDUAL OR ARTIST CRAFTS—made by a few, for a few, at a high price. Consciously made and signed. Examples, Mokubei or Staite Murray.
INDUSTRIAL CRAFTS—such as aluminium saucepans, etc., made under the industrial system by mechanical means.
ARISTOCRATIC CRAFTS—examples, Nabeshima ware in Japan under the patronage of a feudal lord, or Stanley Gibbons in England.
Broadly, such are the divisions.

Q. *Out of all these, which has most craft character?*
A. Folkcraft, especially things made by a community of craftsmen, for that is where you find the purest form of craft. The reason for this is

artist-craftsmanship places utility second and tends to pursue beauty for its own sake, thereby breaking the laws of craftsmanship. Artist-craftsmen separate themselves from the real nature of crafts and approach the fine arts. From the point of view of pure craftsmanship, folkcraft carries the rightful lineage. I do not wish to enter into the discussion at this time of the poverty of material and beauty in most industrial machine-made goods. The *Mishima* wares of Korea are genuine folkcraft, but the individualistic pots by Dōhachi in the *Mishima* style, by approaching fine arts, divide from the main stream.

Q. *Which contain greater beauty, folkcrafts or artist crafts?*
A.   If we place them side by side, strangely enough the artist crafts cannot be said to be better, for they depend upon the personality of the artist rather than the character of the craft. If the names of the artists were unknown, could they have stood the contest? There are people who buy the name of a maker rather than quality. As to aristocratic crafts, in their attention to technique and over-refinement, they, too, are separated from the main stream. It is truly strange that folkcrafts should be better than the work of artists in pursuit of beauty. The works of artist craftsmen are not primarily intended to be just good pots so much as to display the fine sensibility or strength of personality of the maker —the flavour of himself rather than the flavour of mankind, which crafts exude.

Q. *Why is the product of the artist craftsman defeated by the folk craftsman?*
A.   I would like to answer this by saying that "individualistic beauty" is lower than beauty that transcends the individual. To the latter type folkcraft belongs, whereas the individual artist is often so wrapped up in himself and his expression that he goes against the laws of nature. This can also be explained by the fact that the power of the individual is weaker than that of tradition. Personality, however great, is nothing compared with nature. Surprisingly enough, the history of art is full of examples of the products of humble craftsmen that are far finer than the work of clever individuals. This is because their work contains no signs of egotism. It is like looking for true belief in a world infested with self-centredness. Only when egotism diminishes does true belief make an appearance. Just as it is rare to find a sincere man amongst Pharisees, so is it rare to find good work in signed crafts. What artist woodworker has produced furniture to compare with the Gothic? If we were to select a hundred ex-

amples of the most beautiful crafts out of the past and present, ninety-nine percent, no possibly one hundred percent, would be unsigned.

Q. *Are you denying the importance of personality in crafts?*
A. To negate personality is an error; however to remain satisfied with personality is yet a greater error. There is a beauty that emerges from individual art, but it is not purest. In the case of a really great individual, the greatness lies in his having gone beyond his individualism. The reason that the products of artist-craftsmen are found lacking from the standpoint of beauty is because they rarely rise above their individualism. Furthermore, things that are highly individualistic are unsuitable for daily use. The assertion of one individuality is almost sure to produce a clash with another individuality. It is rare to find restfulness in beauty of an individual kind. If in such a way a craft object becomes unsuitable for our daily living, it fails of its purpose. Craftsmanship must not be impeded by individualism.

Stress upon individualism is totally unsatisfactory; on the other hand, where do we find beauty without individualism? Having no individuality and transcending it—these two issues must not be confused.

The virture of folkcrafts is that one feels no obtruding personality in them. The thing shines, not the maker. Consider Persian rugs; one feels their beauty before any question arises as to who made them. Actually, almost any Persian could have made them. The work was subdivided, it was certainly not done by one pair of hands, nor conceived by one mind. Moreover, of these rugs, can any one example be called ugly? Again, let me reiterate that craftsmen must go beyond individualism.

Q. *How does the unlettered craftsman produce beauty?*
A. He may be unlettered, uneducated and lacking any particular force of personality, but it is not from these causes that beauty is produced. He rests in the protecting hand of nature. The beauty of folkcraft is the kind that comes from dependence on the Other Power. Natural material, natural process, and an accepting heart—these are the ingredients necessary at the birth of folkcrafts. Hence it is the kind of beauty that saves us. The craftsman has not the power to save himself. It is nature that does the saving, and therefore whatever is made is lovely. Can we find any ugly or false work amongst folkcrafts? By contrast, if everything depended upon the worker on his own, just think how many mistakes would result. Whereas, left to nature, every piece is saved.

One would be hard pressed to find amongst the myriad artifacts of Gothic craftsmen downright bad work. Likewise in Japanese textiles of the eighth century it would be difficult to find bad colours or patterns.

Q. *Is it not possible for the artist-craftsmen to make beautiful things?*
A. I am not saying that it is absolutely impossible, but it is well to realize that the artist-craftsman's solo path is fraught with difficulty. As long as he lingers in the stage of individualism he can never arrive at the beauty of "no-thought" of folkcraft. To find pure and simple faith in the ranks of intellect is a rarity of rarities. If one wishes to travel by reliance on one's own power, one must pass through great inner discipline akin to that of the Zen monks. Attachment to individualism guarantees no beauty, nor does it even provide the requisite ease in technique. If the way of the individual should become the main stream of craftsmanship, the crafts of the people will suffer. Why? Because the people possess neither a real individuality, nor a real intellect. And yet surprisingly enough it is the crafts of the people that have produced the greatest blossoming. Implicit in this point is the story of how great the difficulty is for the individual. Only a rare genius is able to produce something extraordinary. Today we have individual craftsmen galore. But who can claim that they are all geniuses? A genius may appear once in a generation. The world is already flooded with the works of unenlightened craftsmen.

Q. *What, then, is the value of the artist-craftsman?*
A. If the object of a piece of work is the expression of individualist beauty, then we must admit that the way of craftsmen is limited, for the road of fine arts is better suited for that end. That which ends with individuality does not agree with the nature of craft. In these days of deterioration of the art of the people nobody else is available who can set the standards of beauty other than the artist-craftsman. Today, having our way, we need the capacity of those who can show us how to properly appreciate beauty in work. In the world of crafts we hunger for this leadership. If the artist-craftsman does not rise to this task, our horizons will darken. This phenomenon is required of this age of consciousness. The presence of artist-craftsmen is to serve as a bridge between this period and the next flowering of the art of the people. Their value therefore, lies in their ability to understand beauty rather than in their expression of it. Consequently, their work takes on a great significance as a gift to the world of thought. Unfortunately, so few know clearly what the

target is, and the number of those who have the genius to express true beauty in their work is so limited. Rather, as things are, there are too many who are poisoning the crafts.

In actuality, the artist-craftsman's function is to point the way as a compass does, rather than as a maker. For example, take the case of an artist-potter who makes a pot and puts on it a drawing of a landscape, which is then copied in thousands by many other artisans, as was done in Ming dynasty China. Now the curious thing is that, at the point when awareness of the original dies away, a new beauty far greater than the original comes into being. The object now no longer belongs to the work of the individual but to the craft world of tradition. The work of an artist is thus less than the expression of the people. The value, then, of the individual is principally his contribution to the world of intellectual thought.

Q. *Which is more significant for the future—folk- or artist craft?*
A. The work of the artist-craftsman is to clear the way ahead by pointing in the right direction for the eventual return of craftsmanship to the hands of the people themselves. The ultimate aim is not the expression of the self but to see true beauty, specifically in "people's art". The intent is not to save one individual and his work but to save craftsmen and their work for the future. From the spiritual and from society's point of view, the art of the people as a whole is much more important than the art of any one individual. The decline of folkcraft almost means the death of craftsmanship; such an event would make the Kingdom of Beauty impossible. Confining beauty in the hands of a very few artists is cold comfort. In this situation the artist-craftsman pursuing his lone path of personal integrity is like the hermit of former days. Nevertheless, should not self-purification mean purification of others as well? Hiding away from this world is certainly not the objective. To make a move from the fine arts toward art of the people implies a change from individual salvation to the salvation of society. It is not the task of crafts proper to foster individualism and the individualist approach to work.

Q. *What is to be expected most of the artist-craftsman?*
A. It is to be hoped that the artist-craftsman will awaken to his obligation to contribute beauty to the community. Today this is his greatest failure. As things stand, whatever he does he pursues it with the consciousness of beauty in mind. But the artist of the future needs to be

concerned with the requirements of people around him. The extent to which he contributes to society determines his value. Whilst he holds aloof, leaving the people to their fate, the horrible lampshades remain, benefitting neither him nor society, and so forth. It is far more significant to be saved with others than alone. The trend of social evolution causes one to anticipate the time when artist craftsmen, too, will begin to think of themselves as part of a whole. And the time will come when they will no longer be satisfied to pursue beauty by itself and will cease to be able to turn a cold shoulder upon the art of the people.

Q. *What is lacking in the artist-craftsman?*
A. His products are so few and so expensive. They are more decorative than useful. Even if they are made for use they are expensive and are therefore not employed in daily life, thus becoming luxury items. From the very beginning they are made for art collectors, and become disconnected with the life of the people. The only person who benefits is the favoured purchaser. The artist-craftsman separates himself from need, and thereby divorces himself from the people around him. Is this not a mortal wound to craftsmanship? Apart from use and the people there is no meaning in either craftsmanship or its beauty. If the artist-craftsman continues isolating himself from society, he has a responsibility to admit with humility [out of his own experience] that his position of self-expression is one of insufficiency. And in view of the achievement of the arts of the people, he needs to feel an awakened respect for them and pave the way towards the re-expression of that congregate power. At that moment when the work of the artist-craftsman ceases to be individual and he thus joins the ranks of all men, let him place his work next to the old work that he used to do. And he may see truth for the first time, for his old work will not stand up in service or in beauty.

Q. *What are the strong points in folkcrafts?*
A. They are never made for other than use; they are inexpensive; they are made in quantity sufficient to serve masses of people daily. Their quantity production means repeated practise in their technique, thereby freeing them from ailments arising from artfulness. They are made without obsessive consciousness of beauty; thus we catch a glimpse of what is meant by "no-mindedness", whereby all things become simplified, natural, and without contrivance. These are the qualities that provide a permeance of strength throughout the social and aesthetic edifice. There

are so few evidences of disease in the arts of the people (*getemono*). Rarely are there cases of ugliness to be found in them. The people and their crafts are harmoniously interrelated. How little fine work has come out of intellect, technique, and individuality. By contrast, how little evidence of ugliness there is to be found in those ordinary articles of folk life of the past? This is parallel with Buddhist experience, in which but few Zen monks, relying on their own endeavours, reach true Enlightenment. Whereas amongst the ranks of unlettered, good, simple men and women of Buddhist dependence on Other Power (*tariki*) we find many of profound, humble faith.

Q. *Why do you focus your attention to such an extent on folkcraft?*
A.　(1) My intuition has perceived a far richer beauty in folkcraft than in fine arts. (2) Hitherto in their discussion of crafts almost no one has taken up the contributions of these humble craftsmen and given them their due valuation. (3) Art historians and collectors, on the contrary, have been biased in favour of individual artists. (4) The artist thereby has been kept locked up in his ivory tower of individualism and is out of touch with the people. (5) No one has as yet led the way toward communal expression for crafts. We must bring back the realization of values and those days when all things required in daily, ordinary life were beautiful. Only when we succeed in this can we speak of an epoch of craftsmanship. The beauty of craftsmanship lies with society rather than with the individual. There are many people wanting to be artist-craftsmen, but who is concerned about the improvement of nameless crafts? In fact, nobody believes that it is in this very namelessness that the deep roots of great craft find their sustenance. The only people who are on the increase are those who are fortifying themselves behind castle walls of self-enclosure. Even amongst purchasers, the habit of dependence upon name becomes ever more apparent. The more this habit predominates in the world, the more I feel the need of strengthening the voice of the humble artisan. Unless a wide public takes up this issue, the history of genuine craftsmanship will come to an end.

Q. *Why are the folkcrafts in decline?*
A.　History clearly indicates that as industrial capitalism flourished, handcrafts declined in the East and the West alike. As we look backwards, suddenly in Japan about the year 1887 there was a sharp loss of beauty in all the crafts. Needless to say, this was around the time when

the industrial system surged forward. In the Western world, with the spread of industry, the last of the glory attached to the Middle Ages and its craftsmanship came to an end.

Q. *How does industrial capitalism destroy beauty of folkcraft?*
A. Because the objective of production is profit alone, and even objects' utility is secondary. In front of the eyes of the capitalist is the word "profit". The quality, beauty, and health of an object are all secondary considerations. Greed for profit is destructive of both use and beauty. In addition, under capitalism, craftsmanship leans away from human hands towards machinery. As a consequence, beauty loses its sensibility more and more and tends towards hardness.

Crafts originally sprang from a person's making things for his own use. That was followed by selling for the use of others, and the next stage was the change from handwork to the machine. On the face of things this is a natural evolution, but seen from the other side this process means a change from what was at first healthy into insensibility, from freedom to cold expression, and from kindness to avarice. In this way an age ended that produced almost no ugliness, and a new period was launched where beauty in craft became very difficult. We are now living in a time of severe change.

Q. *Why are today's folkcrafts so impoverished?*
A. Because the capitalist system launches us in a whirlpool of competition, we are forced to use sensational means to attract buyers. The immediate reflection of this is to be seen in bad colours and poor shapes. This bad influence unconsciously affects man's very heart, which is a grave problem. Crafts have lost their lasting values by exchanging them for passing fancy. It is unlikely that the clothes we wear today will ever be displayed in art galleries. This is because they are poor in material and design. Things go on being made that can only be described as bad, and interest lies only in the new and changing. Such an environment fails to deepen the sense of creative imagination, and even the taste of the educated becomes poor.

Q. *What is the effect of industry on crafts?*
A. At present exceedingly bad. As things are, the desire for a world of normal beauty, once more, is unlikely to arise. Although there can be a kind of beauty in things made mechanically, yet nothing so made has

surpassed the beauties of the age of handwork. The shape of things is at present hopeless. Since a tool is a kind of mechanical aid, one cannot say that hand and machine are utterly apart, and, for that matter the hand itself is a machine; why then are things made by hand both more beautiful and more lasting? Actually because it is a freer and more complex machine. However intricate the mechanics of the machine, they are nothing to those of the hand. Man's power is foolish in comparison with nature's.

Artificial dyes can rarely approach vegetable dyes in colour value. What have we that will compare with the tapestry weaving of the eighth century kept in the Hōryū-ji temple?

Q. *Ought we to give up the machine?*
A. Machines are not bad in themselves, but a completely mechanized age would be a disaster. So long as man does not become enslaved to machines he may use them freely. But if machinery is master and man the slave, the effect is disastrous. Broadly seen, however, the more complex the machinery becomes, the more fully men become slaves to it. Man is most free when his tools are proportionate to his needs. At the same time, with the increase in population, work produced by tools, as distinct from machines, ceases to meet demand. We need far more mechanical aid than in earlier times, but man's nature shrinks when this gets too great. We need fresh thought on the problem of how to steer a true course between these two alternatives. The wisest planning would be in the direction of using power in the preparatory stages of work, and the hand in the finishing stages. Handwork would be too wasteful for the one, and machine finish too destructive of quality for the other.

Q. *Has machinery been of great benefit to man?*
A. Yes, it has, but as the economists say, it has also brought poverty. The capitalist system was necessary to the development of mechanization; without it the extension of the use of machines could not have taken place, nor would unemployment have spread. The supply of industrial products has become too great. Machines are not conducive to a happy life. There is a close connection between machines and capitalism. Capitalism lives on commerce and produces competition in machine-made goods. The use of machines reduces the time of production, but the things so made are less good, the workers less happy and often out of work, and too often the worker cannot buy what he makes. Altogether,

although the machine may have brought some benefits, the real loss is far greater.

Q.   *How can we lessen the amount of mechanization?*
A.   If high profits were cut, the whole system would become self-controlled, the haphazard proliferation of factories would automatically cease, and, proportionately, the demand for quality, involving more handwork, would increase, and the greater understanding of and desire for handwork would grow.

Q.   *Would it not be going backwards to reject what we have gained through mechanization?*
A.   We must arrest the harm that is being done by misuse of machines. In the peace following a war mankind does not wish to preserve the worst weapons of destruction. Does one object to having one's appendix removed? I am not proposing the rejection of the machine, but I am saying that we must curb the unlimited spread of that mechanization that brings with it loss of beauty, bad products, and bad conditions of life. There are many who believe that greater mechanization improves life, but they judge from a scientific point of view, disregarding the quality and beauty of artifacts. What machine-made article for home life is more beautiful than one made by hand? We must not confuse admiration for the machine itself with an automatic satisfaction with its products.

Q.   *Are handcrafts not out of date?*
A.   I do not think so. They are not against the machine. Where mechanization can dovetail with handwork it is of obvious benefit to man, but where it destroys the values in the work of the human hand it is downright stupid. Handwork, because it has nature behind it, has a way of fostering good life. It is too hasty to assume that with the close of the tool age, handwork has ceased to have importance. That is the equivalent of saying that with the birth of science, religion has ceased to have meaning. No matter how far science advances, religion retains its meaning; more so, in fact. There is no change in the basic importance of the hand or its work. The cry for hand work will arise again and again.

Q.   *Can a greater content of beauty be obtained in machine-made goods?*
A.   Certainly, to a point. But there is a definite limit. That limit is at the point of mechanical repetition, where freedom of expression stops, making the expression of beauty most difficult. To obtain more beauty out of

the whole process requires more release of the human spirit in it. This limit is born of the profit motive in capitalism. In that world, profit matters, not beauty for its own fair face. To introduce beauty as an adjunct is quite hazardous.

Q. *How, then, can we resuscitate living craftsmanship?*
A. It would be most difficult without a change in the social system. Under present conditions folkcrafts are dying, bad factory products are increasing, and the artist-craftsman works for the collector. Here and there pockets of traditional crafts can be found, a thin trickle from a healthy past. Whenever I see them, the desire rises in me to help them, but it is a difficult task as things stand. I am keenly aware of the urgent need for a social change.

Q. *What system do you consider necessary for folk art?*
A. In my opinion, now that capitalism has killed handcrafts, the only way is through the guild system. The finest crafts of the past were produced under it. Guilds and crafts were inseparable. Beautiful crafts were the outcome of the co-operation between craftsmen.

Q. *What are guilds?*
A. Associations for mutual help and preserving order. Order involves basic morality. The morality guaranteed the quality of the products. It gave the work its character, guaranteed its craftsmanship, and refused to allow bad work to be sold. From the character and quality of the resultant work, social confidence was established and the craftsmen themselves were supported and encouraged. Without moral order amongst craftsmen decay sets in. Contrast this with our present civilization, with its basis in private profit and uncontrolled over-production of inferior goods.

Q. *What would be the effect of guilds on the beauty of crafts?*
A. Guild life discourages egotism, therefore its crafts would supersede individualist crafts. Instead of spasmodic expression, ordered expression would result—the beauty of unity instead of individualistic crafts. This change would lead to the expression of the people, to a new epoch, which means entry into the Kingdom of Beauty. Examples from the past may be found in European Medieval and Sung Chinese crafts in which, instead of individualist beauty, communal beauty pervades and saves all. In those epochs there was practically no ugliness, is that not astounding? Without guilds how else could such a kingdom be reached?

208

Q. *What would be the feasible aims of such guilds?*
A.   At present the common aim is the expression of personality. But in the new guilds, as in the old, the expression would be that of humanity, the will to live and work together, not as a means to an end, but as an end in itself. There is no other rational answer. From this guild seed, the tree can grow. It is a universal idea with a Messianic meaning. Without this I see no hope of a rebirth of the arts of the people—the crafts. Religion teaches that without a church there is no salvation. I feel in this a very profound truth.

Q. *Is there a hope for revival of folk art?*
A.   I have not abandoned hope, but I have but little hope under the existing order, for it does not recognize truth and beauty, and it is perfectly clear that from a religious, a moral, or even an economic way, the present capitalist system is untenable. Whatever happens, the change towards better social conditions will not be arrested. Beyond and above social change I can see the beacon light of a Kingdom of Beauty. A recent and remarkable phenomenon has been the increased interest in the Middle Ages and especially in its guild socialism.

Some critics feel that this is a regrettable retreat into the past, but I feel that, although it may appear to them as a retracing of footsteps, in fact it is a rediscovery of social truth of a permanent order. It is unimportant if guilds are old or new.

Q. *Should the social order alter, could one expect a quick blossoming of beauty?*
A.   That is too simple. The rank and file of humanity has submitted to a twisted order for so long that beauty is a stranger. People no longer respond spontaneously to beauty and ugliness. One cannot expect a sudden outpouring of beauty from such a condition.

Q. *Where do we find the standard of beauty?*
A.   We must take a fresh look at real folkcraft of the past, for it is there that we may find healthy and genuine beauty expressed. We must learn from such examples what law is at work that causes us to recognize inevitable beauty.

Q. *Does this not mean mere inheritance of past procedures?*
A.   To reflect upon the past does not mean that we should automatically rest in old procedures. It is only normal to vary reactions to changing

conditions. However, the principles that yield beauty in crafts are un-changing and timeless. We do not admire work because of the past but because of its enduring present. This surrender of oneself before beauty is for its eternity. Is it not true that, regardless of time, things of great beauty reawaken fresh life? In fact, we cannot acclaim works that are defeated by time.

Q. *In what type of former crafts do we find the most healthy kind of beauty revealed?*
A.   Rather than in precious and refined forms of art, it is amongst the odds and ends of things hitherto scorned or derided, amongst objects of unstressed and ordinary everyday life (*getemono*), that the norm of health may be found. By health, I mean to point at the honest quality, the form and feeling that is in full accord with use, which is the very seeing eye of craft. The bad handling of material, the over-complicated procedures of technique, over-employment of decoration, slick skills, one-sidedness of personality, over-self-consciousness—these are all forms of disease for the simple reason that they do not fit the purpose of use. In refined wares such abnormalities are often in evidence, whereas in com-mon, everyday things such are exceedingly rare. Up to the present, refinement has been equated with beauty, but to think that technical skill is immediately connected with beauty is an impoverished way of evalua-tion. In seeking healthy beauty, we must of necessity enter the domain of the everyday wares of good periods of handcraftsmanship.

Q. *What is meant by* getemono?
A.   *Ge* means "ordinary" or "common", and *te* means "by nature". That is to say, *nami no mono*, "something of a quite practical nature".
[In Japanese this word does not mean what we Westerners would mean, because the everyday article with us is machine made, whereas in Japan many things are still made by hand and are thereby capable of humanly expressive beauty. This implies, on the one hand, that the machine, being what it is, a reduplicator, cannot at most do more than freeze an instant of creative life, and on the other, that the human hand is guided by creative mind; in other words the hand is capable of a far greater degree of spirit in matter. In Japan the word *getemono*, though having a derogatory overtone, applies to common household objects made by hand, the appreciation of which is still traditionally alive in the best sense.—B. L.].

I find it an astonishing providence that in these unsigned, cheap, abundant, quite ordinary articles there so often lies hidden a beauty that one could hardly expect to discover. The uncovering of this truth is a great affirmation of the common man. It bespeaks the total harmony between the concepts of economy and aesthetics.

Q. *Are you stating that in* getemono *alone one discovers the beauty of craftsmanship?*
A. No, I am not arriving at such a crude conclusion, for even in fine crafts what is beautiful is beautiful. But we must note that in fine crafts the examples of beauty are extremely rare, and even in them the expression or the state of mind from which they sprang stands upon the same basis as that of the *getemono*: there must be neither over-calculation nor complexity; the direct response to innate nature, naturalness, and simplicity are seen therein. But after all, are these not the very qualities of the beauty of the *getemono?* Here we may see how closely the perception of beauty in *getemono* and in crafts is connected. We have come all this way without clarification of this truth. In contrast to the habitual way of thinking that beauty in crafts is almost always dependent upon refinement, this view may bring about a reversal of values.

Q. *Why do fine crafts so often fail?*
A. To the extent to which they become separate from use, they are stripped of craftsmanlike content. The nearer to uselessness, the nearer to sickness. They seldom escape from the affliction of self-consciousness. They fall so easily into the pitfall of themselves. The craftsman is apt to become over-anxious about sheer skill. Thus the increase of complexity, additional decor, and self-conscious effort all become accentuated. Not only do fine crafts remove themselves from use by pursuing artistry, but they do not even fill demand, because their output becomes less. Consequently, the article becomes expensive, and economic problems arise. Surrounded by such sick conditions, the production of healthy articles diminishes. Fine wares are generally meant for admiration in a glass case, and, not being intended for use, they of necessity lack constructive strength. We cannot find in such things the main flow of craftsmanship.

Q. *Why is healthy beauty more richly manifest in* getemono *than in fine crafts?*
A. *Getemono* are things that work and serve us from day to day, not

211

things kept in a glass case merely to be looked at. Their role is work, and therefore they do not lean towards frivolity. The worker must be sober in look and strong of body. If the body is weak, one cannot work: health is a natural requisite to perform work properly. In this obvious fact lies such objects' honest, simple, humble beauty. To reiterate, the principle of craftsmanship, where beauty and use are perfectly equated, may be found before one's eyes, like the thumb and fingers of one hand. Where else can we find greater beauty, in which naturalness, balance, and stability predominate?

Q. *Up until now has anyone deeply appreciated the significant beauty of getemono?*
A. We would like to draw attention to the early men of Tea, such as those who are recognized as great masters, Murata Shukō, Takeno Jōō, Sen no Rikyū, and Sōami, and, somewhat later, Honami Kōetsu, too, may be included. Nobody in the world has ever so appreciated or fostered the beauty to be discovered in such crafts. One may say that the exceptional love for crafts of the Japanese people has been mothered in the Way of Tea.

Q. *Why do you lay stress upon the early masters of Tea?*
A. Because from approximately the middle of the history of Tea onwards, including Tea of the present day, the criteria have become a movement shunted from behind. The intuitive creative process has dried up. Only formalism remains. The decay began about the time of Kobori Enshū (1579–1647), and now Tea has sunk into the mud of bad taste and cannot save itself. The most serious result for crafts has been the mistaken men of Tea who are today incapable of appreciating the true crafts and have become its worst enemies.

Q. *In what direction lay the greatness of the early Tea masters?*
A. In the freedom of their creative intuition: by their ability to see and seize upon the astonishing beauty laying latent and awaiting them in the world of miscellaneous articles that nobody particularly noticed. No one ever had as sharp eyes as they had to see the aesthetic value of folkcraft. They chose nothing but *getemono* for their Tea. Those *ō-meibutsu*, or great masterpieces, were no more than common *getemono* costing but a few pennies. Tea-rooms they may be called, but in fact they were based upon simple peasant cottages. The early masters perceived in the world

of folkcraft the highest expression of beauty. The beauty of *shibusa*, of subtle, noble austerity, of *gen*, depth after depth. They played in the world of *gen* in silent samadhi. The Way of Tea is the religion of beauty. They savoured the beauty of Holy Poverty. When appreciation reaches this height, it is Life Itself.

Q. *Is there room for Tea to develop further?*
A. With certitude I reply. Tea contains the principle from which all beauty derives. However, this principle is a living spirit and not a dead body. As soon as the principle becomes formalized, death approaches. The greatness of those Tea masters lay in their free employment of this principle. If there is any life to be found in the Way of Tea, there lies an open road ahead of us for its further development. Where creative intuition is involved, there are no bounds. For instance, we of today are surrounded by countless examples of *getemono* that the early masters never had the opportunity to see. We are now able to select new Tea implements from anywhere. We might even apply Tea to a modern way of living. There is no need to follow the old proportions and construction of Tea-rooms and the things used in them. It is precisely such a freedom that the old Tea masters taught. We are endowed with the freedom to select any number of *ō-meibutsu* for ourselves. Not to be able to recognize unlabeled beauty of the same standard of the great masterpieces, born as they were out of the same principles as famous old pieces, is due to the sad poverty of intuition and the eyes with which to see. For myself, I am astonished to discover the treasure trove of things in this category. Furthermore, I am amazed to see how many such articles are cast aside unrecognized. We are fortunate to be living in an epoch giving far richer opportunities than in the times of the early Tea masters.

Q. *Do you find that the outlook of the early Tea masters regarding the beauty of craft was in any way deficient?*
A. Those men of Tea savoured implements from the point of view of beauty; but although their outlook may be called depth in appreciation, it cannot be called depth of *cognition* for those of us who live in a conscious age. Together with seeing beauty, we want to understand the truth behind it. We are concerned with the principles that cause beauty. Especially today, we reflect upon the social background that made such beauty possible. We do not remain on the level of appreciation alone, for we are urged on in the search for truth. Thus our observation of the past

leads us on towards a creative future. We are kept far busier than the early people of Tea.

Q. *Are* getemono *anything more than rough and primitive?*
A.   *Getemono* are the very things that are likely to satisfy the highest developed perception, because they contain the beauty of *shibusa* and of "no-thought". They are representations of nature itself. We cannot expect to find a deeper beauty anywhere. Some may say they are rough because they derive directly from nature, yet there is no higher intelligence than in the workings of nature. By contrast, how many examples of refined wares can we discover that have reached the sphere of *shibusa*? Such objects exist in the realm of "thought"—they are the products of wilful endeavour, they run towards opulent display, and drown in individualism. In this process nature is destroyed. At a glance they may be gorgeous, but one soon tires of them. Some may say these are works of man's ingenuity, but before the face of nature how crude and immature they are.

Q. *Is it not the obligation of the future to base crafts upon the development of science?*
A.   It is not for us to ignore or discredit science. But are we not giving it too much to do? In fact, if we look at the products of science and compare them with those of the past, we will not be able to discover one that is beautiful. Nor is this position likely to change, because science works in a finite sphere. St. Paul said, "Man's wisdom is foolishness before God", and the same can be said before nature. Scientifically made things contain the interest inherent in intellect, but intellect is not synonymous with beauty. In fact it usually destroys beauty. The idea that science can overrule nature is the most arrogant, crude, and empty concept imaginable. We must not ignore intellect, nor must we overlook the limitations of the intellect. Is there a greater wisdom than nature's, which outstrips anything that man can conceive? Knowledge of the deepest order is to be described as that which is in accordance with nature. A good product of science, then, is not the result of conquest but a tribute to nature's greatness.

Q. *What is the meaning of placing such importance on nature?*
A.   First, nature must be freely at work in the mind when anything is well made. Though painstaking efforts may have their contribution to make in carrying out a work, more astonishing is the effect that "no-

mindedness" has upon it. One gains greater insight into nature by open trust rather by attempts at intellectual understanding.

Secondly, procedures must be natural. Nature's simplicity hides a greater complexity than man's. Beauty requires neither indirectness nor intricacy. Try to add or contrive, and life vanishes. Great detail and high finish have to do with technique but have nothing to do directly with beauty. In fact, they interfere with it. Lovely things are almost always simply made.

Thirdly, the material provided by nature is nearly always best. Nothing is more precious than the unspoiled character of raw material. For it is always richer than the man-made. Man thinks that artificial material [such as glass] is pure, but from nature's side it is impure and forced. When we think back on great periods, we can almost say the material is synonymous with craftsmanship. One aspect of the beauty of crafts lies in the beauty of the materials. May we not accept crafts as generally being local? Crafts are born where the necessary raw materials are found. The closer we are to nature the safer we are; the further away, the more dangerous.

Q. *What is the fundamental principle of the beauty of craft?*
A.   The principle of the beauty of craft is no different from the law that rules the spirit underlying all things. There is then no truer source than the words of the religious scriptures. A true example of craft is the same as a passage of a holy scripture. Only in place of words, truth is conveyed through material, shape, colour, and pattern. Gothic crafts and Gothic religious spirit spoke with the same voice. It is also this same spiritual law that one sees expressed in the crafts of the Sung dynasty. Even in one single piece of good work, one finds expounded in material form the commandment to refrain from attaching oneself to the ego, the heart of Zen, which teaches "no-thought", the standpoint of the Other Power (*tariki*) school, which embraces and saves all beings without exception. Faith and beauty are but different aspects of the Absolute Reality.

I hope with these lines I have been able to express very nearly what I mean by craft.

1927

The Responsibility of the Craftsman

When the Great Reason is obliterated,
We have benevolence and justice.
When wisdom and sagacity appear,
We have much hypocrisy.
When family relations are no longer harmonious,
We have filial piety and paternal love.
When a nation is in disorder,
We have loyalty and allegiance.

Laotze

I think there is significant truth in this saying. The fact that a great moralist appears in this world is nothing but the evidence of immorality prevailing on the earth. He has to rise against the immorality. In other words, though it may sound a little cynical, he appears in this world on account of its immorality, that is, if the world were completely virtuous, he would have little chance to make himself famous. He is respected and esteemed highly on account of unvirtuous circumstances. We look with admiration and respect on a sublime moralist. But does it really mean we are happy to have such a moralist in this world? It is true we are thankful to him; and our life will be unhappy and restless unless the moralist is born. But is he required at all times? No, only when the world lacks morality. We wouldn't need him particularly if morality were common and a usual thing in this world. And if he in such a state endeavours to reform the world, it would be funny indeed that a moralist teaches morality to a world that needs no moralist at all. The fact that he is noted on the earth is the mere proof that the world is in unhappy disorder. A doctor cannot live unless he has patients, while the ideal of medical art is to decrease their number. Therefore we, mankind, have paid an unreasonably expensive bill to get a Socrates. That is why Laotze said, "Wisdom and sagacity appear, and we have much hypocrisy." It seems well said. Loyalty and filial piety are highly esteemed in Confucianism, but we should praise the world that needs no loyalty and filial piety, shouldn't we? Call me dreaming a fantastic dream or talking about Utopia, if you like, but you cannot deny that the world badly needs great moralists and great philosophers, for it is getting worse and worse.

Today, many artists gather here to think about improvement and progress of crafts. And what is the need of it? It is because the world of crafts has so much degraded as to need a meeting. Not only in Europe and America, but in the Orient as well such circumstances are seen. Unless conscientious and able artists or craftsmen rise and do their best work, the world of crafts will be threatened with the peril of stagnation and become dull and cold.

Especially in Europe, traditional manual work has been obliterated since the Industrial Revolution. By reason of the machine industry, which took the place of manual work, there have been few products that are really human. This is due not only to the limitations of their mechanisms but also to the fact that machines are used by commercial interests to make enormous profit.

In America, since it is a young country having not much tradition, almost all articles are made by machines. Of course, some of the machine-made things are quite good, yet there are many defects, which have been well acknowledged even by Americans. Comparing machine-made articles with handmade, it is natural that people come to desire the various excellent qualities that are special attributes of handcrafts, and consider the world "handmade" as synonymous to "good quality".

There are three elements that are specially required in the sphere of crafts. First, a large number of conscientious individual artists in handcrafts is especially needed. Next, the importance and value of such craftsmen should be widely acknowledged and respected by society. And, third, intense co-operation should be considered between the individual artists and industrialists of machine production.

The first element—that conscientious artists should emerge now—is to protect the beauty of craft. They may be compared with moralists in

217

immoral times. Our life would be abominable if we had no artists in this world. Therefore, an artist should be a proper appreciator of beauty, also its creator, and, in a word, a genius. Our aesthetic culture will improve to the extent that such active men of genius appear.

The degradation of quality is found not only in mechanical products but also in handmade products of the Orient, where traditional crafts have thriven in the past. It is entirely a sacrifice to mercantilism by the wholesale dealers. Artisans as a whole are economically subordinate to wholesale dealers who pay as little as possible in order to get big margins of profit. Low quality articles gradually increase in this way. Conscientious artists are needed in the Orient, just as in Europe.

But in proportion to the importance of their duty and responsibility, their work will be very difficult. They must be qualified with: the right sensibility towards beauty; sufficient technical training; scientific knowledge, which is indispensable to crafts; strong will and passion; creative talent.

Because of the difficulty of fulfilling all these conditions at the same time, we cannot expect many excellent individual artists. Statistics will tell us strictly there are few geniuses on the eartn.

Especially in Europe and America, where there are few vestiges of tradition in the sphere of handcrafts, it seems most difficult to work. The artists have to do everything themselves and often have to improvise or use indirect methods for whatever they make. Artists in Japan, on the contrary, are much blessed. They still have tradition, proper materials, which are easily obtainable, many artisans who are able to assist them, and many good traditional patterns. For instance, in Japan perhaps more than four thousand handcraft pottery kilns are active today. In spite of favourable conditions, the fact that we have only a few artists in Japan can only be explained by their rarity anywhere.

However, as I stated before, whether artists can do good work or not depends chiefly upon society. Both in Europe and America for a long time painters and sculptors have been socially acknowledged as "artists". It is only recently that craftsmen also have received the same recognition. It is quite doubtful if people in general look at a pot with the same respect as they do at a painting. Without the recognition of society even the greatest artist cannot do sufficient work, because he has to face constant economic anxiety. Accordingly, attempts to improve the attitude of society through aesthetic and cultural education at school is very important. School education these days seems to be inclined too much to intellect and is lacking in cultural feeling.

Compared to occidental countries, Japan is in a very blessed social condition in respect to the arts of pottery. Japan may be a paradise for potters: people have a special inclination and regard for ceramics, there are a great number of collectors, and publications about pottery have never failed to sell. The reasons for this are found in the country's traditions and culture. The Tea ceremony in Japan has taught many generations how to choose and use the proper Tea utensils. It also has brought some defects: even the second- and third-rate pottery craftsmen can live fairly well in Japan. There may be many who wish to be the patrons of craftsmen. But the duty and responsibility of craftsmen in society should not be limited just to making good products, or to holding their own exhibitions, or to permitting their products to be bought by collectors; they should also do something directly connected with society. Therefore it is natural that a closer relationship between machine products and craftsmen should come about.

Considering the future, handmade products alone are not able to meet the demand of the rapidly increasing population and also the necessity to make the price as cheap as possible. Consequently it is desirable for artists to have some connection with machine production in order to reform and improve its quality. In machine production, designers decide everything. If they are excellent, we will have excellent productions, and if not, low quality will be the result. In making articles by machines, artisans have little or no privilege to select the materials as well as the designs. They are only there to work according to the decisions already made. There is no chance for them to apply any originality. Therefore, it is necessary first of all to employ excellent designers. That has been, to tell the truth, hardly realized, at least in Japan. Neither industrialists nor employers have real understanding of beauty. They scarcely let the designers work freely. Companies should recognize the high position of the designers and pay them well. But the fact is, which I greatly regret, mercantilism oppresses and restricts their designs. The most desirable thing is that their freedom and originality should be applied with mutual confidence. While the designers' responsibility is very important, they should remember all the time that if their designs are not right they commit the sin of sending many wrong products to society. They should not neglect scientific knowledge, thereby failing to distinguish the function of machines, the quality of materials, the aim of products, and the natural forms and colours that are proper for the machine to produce. They should carefully avoid, for instance, the forms that are difficult to make by machine and designs that are unsuitable for some materials. They should also avoid unworthy products and too expensive methods of production. Rather, they should, naturally, endeavour to produce articles that are pleasant to the eyes, practically useful, and helpful as our daily companions to create a happy life.

Today the artist characteristically does his work individually and finds freedom in his individuality. But an artist in the future should have the social consciousness to supply social demand; mechanical industry needs his co-operation. In the Oriental countries, where many handcrafts from ancient times are still in existence, the individual artist has the responsibility of leadership, guidance, and protection of many artisans of towns and villages. In other words, the individual artist should feel that his new mission is to work together with many other artisans. Though the work that no one but he can produce naturally has its value, nevertheless the essential aspect of practical art is to be found in the presentation of the individual artist together with many other artisans. To absorb the individual character in a union of artisans, or in other words, to revive the individual artist in a united co-operation will be necessary. We call him the individual artist because he generally lives by himself, but the artist in the future should sometimes live outside of his ivory tower. His final object should be, I think, to live among people, not to live alone forever.

Interpreting the words of Laotze, the world needs an artist lest darkness prevail. The one who brings the light into a degenerated age is the artist, and as he does so he performs a mission. But the world that does not require the special individual artist is a wonderful world—a world where the genius is merely a common individual. I think such a world is a place of the greatest virtue—nor is it only a dream. Let us take the beauty of Sung pottery for example. The Sung wares were not made by a few distinguished geniuses. All pottery of the Sung age was made by unknown artisans. Not any of this pottery was made by an individual artist as in these days. Everyone made wonderful pottery—genius was found everywhere. The word genius had not yet been invented. No one had reason to admire the single, individual artist. Sung wares were made in such a wonderful age; they have won the greatest admiration, and, incidentally, an unreasonable price, today.

What is the power that protects and puts such great value on these wares? It is not the power of the individual, but something above and beyond that gives this protection. One might say that the Sung potters relied entirely upon grace given by heaven. This grace was tradition, surroundings, and their materials, each beyond the power of the individual. The beauty of their wares was gained and assured by accepting these blessings. Most ordinary artisans, and poor men and women without any education, or sometimes even old people and young children produced wonderful work merely because they readily accepted these blessings. If they had rebelled against them, they would instantly have fallen into distressing circumstances, for they were weak and powerless in their society. It is very significant that many progressive pottery craftsmen at the present time consider the Sung wares as their models. But these modern craftsmen must endure many difficulties, while it was easy for the old Sung craftsmen to produce such wonderful work. What is the reason? The reason is that no individual artist today is living in his proper environment. When tradition has decayed, only the genius is left at work. This is not a fortunate condition at all.

Once tradition has died out, it is necessary for individual artists to work in place of the tradition. Their purpose, however, must not be to work for themselves or by themselves, but to prepare the way to make a new tradition. For that reason it is desirable that they have strong social consciousness. Otherwise society around them is not helped, even though they attain a personal salvation. Without social salvation the kingdom of crafts shall not prosper. The difference between the mission of a pure artist and that of craftsmen will always focus around this point. Of the former it will be said that he goes his own way, while of the latter that he readily goes together with society. Furthermore in seeking the essential meaning of crafts, it should be remembered that craft objects are widely used, rather than widely appreciated. I think any work of art should not be separate from practical use, but rather harmonize with it. Then its beauty will be truly displayed. It may well be the craftsmen's duty to enhance the practical beauty of goods, rather than only to make goods of practical use beautiful. But if craft objects are made only for appreciation, their existence will naturally be unsound. Craft plays an important role in the Kingdom of Beauty of this world: its products have a close relationship with the daily life of common people; because they are closely related with people's lives they are of practical use, and this usefulness is important accordingly. Let us not forget the beauty of Sung pottery. It was not produced only for beauty's sake, but was made for use. Yes, because of this character of usefulness, craft is firm and special in comparison with pure fine art.

When the work of an artist has developed properly, he need not worry about recognition by others; also, naturally his work will not need his signature. Peacefully he will make things, though nobody will ask the name of the maker. If he must say occasionally, "I made this and this", then his circumstances are not yet such as will promise him true happiness. The most beautiful work will be completed when the artist entirely absorbs himself and his honour in his work. It does not mean killing himself; on the contrary, it is the best way to keep alive. But if he sticks to himself or is restrained in some way or another, he cannot freely make his objects nor give them true meaning. Without freedom there is no beauty. Beauty will be accomplished only when complete freedom is acquired. Most of the artist-craftsmen are the slaves of artistry.

Almost all craftsmen believe that they deserve the honour of signing their names on their wares because they call themselves individual artists. Their customers and critics, too, appreciate things with signatures on them. Gradually the public begins to respect these signed works because they are made by artists, and interest in objects without signatures wanes. Prices of objects often depend upon the existence of signatures. Even if there are no signatures on them, critics and historians will reveal and record who the makers are. These records become very important, because they determine the value of the objects, set customers' minds at ease, and raise the market price. We may call these modern times the Age of Signatures or the Age of Attribution. This is the age when artists are acknowledged as heroes in the craft world.

Does this provide a solution, and will this age of the individual artist promise the world a great happiness? I am one who thinks not; the need for a hero is merely one of the phenomena in the age of individualism. People may need a hero at any time, as history necessarily shows, but as Laotze said before, this need is caused by the unhappiness of the age.

When I was a student, I read Carlyle's *Heroes and Hero Worship* and Emerson's *Representative Men*. These books present the ideas of the nineteenth century; nevertheless, perhaps the ideas may have much value at any time. Hero worship may happen when the world is full of people who are not heroes and at such a time as the world has no social happiness. When heroes are not needed, when they become ordinary people and their existence is not uncommon—then the times are most admirable.

I have never seen even a single bad fifth century Egyptian Coptic or ancient Peruvian textile. Every piece is very beautiful. No matter how beautiful, they are never signed. They were not made by heroes. Such circumstances are ideal.

Signing one's name on one's product is not wrong, but from the viewpoint of Oriental religion, it reveals the act of attachment. An artist signs to advertise himself through his work. But are there any circumstances when the artist entirely forgets himself and makes his work shine brilliantly, when his work speaks for him instead of propping him up? Briefly, the things made are themselves the best signature; his inscription or seal is not needed on them. He need not advertise his name; his work will speak for him. We cannot imagine a finer circumstance than when the artist shines as brilliantly as this. When potters admire the Sung pots, they wish to be makers of similar beautiful wares. Yet everyone knows that Sung pottery is without signatures. One of the essential causes of the beauty of Sung pots lies in their anonymity. The objects themselves are a better assurance than any signature could give. The problem of craft cannot be solved entirely by craftsmen's individual work.

In Japan, where many individual artists have appeared for a long time, it is now a great problem for them to make objects in any other way. In a word, they should brighten their works rather than themselves, remove all the honour from themselves, thus making their pieces honourable. And, as in religion, a real salvation is found in the field of craft—one finally finds real self-affirmation in the abandonment of self.

Modern fine art may be established in individuality, but craftsmen in the present times should live in society and think of the essential character of craftsmanship. Let us give cheers for that age when again many beautiful unsigned goods are produced. I look forward to the time when again such beautiful goods are used as a matter of course in daily life. It will be the golden age of craft when many beautiful things are sold cheaply. If there is a reason for the existence of individual artists, it is that they prepare for the realization of such an age. The happiness of society is not to be stabilized in individual work itself.

The fact that there really have been many periods when beautiful unsigned goods were sold cheaply and widely used implies that individual artists should look more freely from their narrow road to a broad highway. In Japan the greatest problem is to set the individual artist free from his individuality. Japan is suffering from the flood of too many worthless artists. She is also suffering because objects made by second- and third-rate artists are selling well. This is due to the excess admiration of signed goods. Shōji Hamada and the late Kanjirō Kawai do not put their signatures on their pieces. It is really the first significant phenomenon in history among individual artists. When someone asked Kawai, "Why do you not sign your name on your work?" he said, "My work itself is my best signature". Hamada was asked the same question. His answer was, "I will make things to be used without the question of who has made them". Both of them naturally are earnest admirers of old unsigned crafts.

Hamada has two kilns, one is small, the other large. The latter is so large that it can contain about ten thousand pots. When he built it, someone asked him, "Why do you need such a large kiln? What are you going to do with it?"

His answer was something like this:

"If a kiln is small, I might be able to control it completely, that is to say, my own self can become a controller, a master of the kiln. But man's own self is but a small thing after all. When I work at the large kiln, the power of my own self becomes so feeble that it cannot control it adequately. It means that for the large kiln, the power that is beyond me is necessary. Without the mercy of such invisible power I cannot get good pieces. One of the reasons why I wanted to have a large kiln is because I want to be a potter, if I may, who works more in grace than in his own power. You know nearly all the best old pots were done in huge kilns".

1952

Index

Abiko, 88, 94, 97
Amitabha, 136, 141, 142
Aquinas, St. Thomas, 110
Aphrodite of Melos, 151
architecture, 102, 161-64
Ashikaga period (1333-1573), 104, 165
awamori, 170

banana fibre, 169
batik, 118, 167
Bible, 141
bingata: Okinawan stencil dyeing, 166, 167, *Pl. 7*
Black Ships, 91
Blake and Whitman, 10, 93
Blake, Beth, 103
Blake, William, 9, 89, 93, 141
Bodhidharma, 138, *Pl. 42*
Bon festival, 165
Browne, Sir Thomas, 140
Buddhism, 9, 92, 99, 103, 104, 121, 127-57
buji: "No event(s)"; denotes total spiritual freedom, self-sufficiency, 139
bunan: "Without difficulty"; close to *muge* in meaning, 139

capitalism, 168, 205, 206, 208
Carlyle, Thomas, 149, 222
celadons, Koryo dynasty, 132, 142
Cezanne, Paul, 93
Chang-an, 152

Chao-chou Ts'ung-shen (778-897), T'ang dynasty Zen master, 137, 138
Chartres Cathedral, 88
China, 116, 125, 132, 138, 158, 161, 190, 196, 202, 208
Christianity, 127, 141, 148, 149
Communism, 104
Confucius, 188
Coptic textiles, 136, 223, *Pl. 27*
crests, family, 113, *Pl. 23*

dance, Okinawan, 164, 165
Da Vinci, Leonardo, 146
Denmark, 96, 97, 108
Diamond Sutra, 146
Dōhachi (1783-1855): Kyoto potter known for overglaze enamel work, 199
dyeing, textile, 118, 166, 167, *Pls. 7, 72*

Eames, Charles, 95-97
Eckhart, Meister, 89, 93, 146
Einfühlungstheorie, 152
Emerson, Ralph Waldo, 222
England, 87, 107
Enneads, 146
Europe, 10, 107, 116, 124, 159, 208, 217, 218

Folkcraft Museum, Japan, 90, 95, 99, 101, 102, 105, 106, 108, 196
Fourfold Vision, 93
funi: "Non-duality"; the state before differentiation occurs, 127
fusoku furi: "neither attached nor non-attached"; denotes true freedom, 146

getemono: "common things", 204, 210-14
Giotto, 93
Gothic crafts, 198, 199, 201, 208, 209, 215
Greece, 124
guild system, 198, 208, 209

hakeme, 139, 171-76, *Pl. 4*
Hamada, Shōji, 87, 89, 91, 94-96, 98, 99, 101, 102, 176, 224, *Pl. 76*
Heroes and Hero Worship, 222
Himeji castle, 161
Hisamatsu, Shin'ichi, 121
hon-kawarabuki: roofs constructed of alternate flat and circular tiles, 163
Honami Kōetsu, 125, 194, 212
Honda Tadayoshi, 190
Hsiang-yen Chih-hsien: T'ang dynasty Zen master, 150

Hung-jen (605–675): The Fifth Chinese Patriarch of Zen, 140, 157
Hui-neng (637–713): The Sixth Chinese Patriarch of Zen, 140, 157

Ido Tea-bowls, 98, 125, 190–96, *Pl. 1*
igyō-dō: "The Easy Way"; reliance on the grace of the Buddha, 133
ikat: Indonesian warp-dyed textile, 168
Industrial Revolution, 87, 90, 96, 107, 217
Inuyama enameled stoneware, 169

Jesus Christ, 127, 131, 141, 193
jiriki: "Self Power"; attaining Enlightenment through self effort, 10, 125, 132
Jishū: A Japanese sect of Pure Land Buddhism, 10
Jōdo Shinshū: A Japanese sect of Pure Land Buddhism founded by Shinran, 10
John, Gospel of, 131

Kabir, 131
Kamakura period (1185–1333), 104
Kangso, Korea, 160
Kanzan (1277–1360): A Japanese priest of the Rinzai Zen sect, 128
kasuri: Warp- and weft-dyed textiles, 118, 168, *Pls. 2, 30, 31*
Kawai, Kanjirō, 94, 98, 101, 176, 191, 224
kenshō: "One's own true nature seen"; Buddhist Enlightenment experience, 152
Kenzan VI, 94
kōan, 172, 196
Kobori Enshū (1579–1647), 212
Kōgei, 94
Kohō-an, 191, 193
Korea, 10, 87, 94, 97–99, 101, 116, 121–23, 125, 132, 142, 160, 163, 170–76, 191, 199
Koryo dynasty (936–1392), 101, 132, 142
Kōya-san, 94, 101
Kuei-shan Ling-yu (771–853): T'ang dynasty Zen master, 129
kumi-odori: Group dances of Okinawa, 165
Kyoto, 161, 162

lacquer, 118, *Pls. 8, 12, 25, 34, 37, 40*
Laotze, 141, 216, 217, 220, 222
lathe work, Korean, 122, 123, *Pl. 37*
Lipps, Theodor, 152
literati, 120

Mason, J. W. T., 92
Matisse, Henri, 119
Ma-tsu Tao-i (d. 788): T'ang dynasty Zen master, 145

Matsudaira Fumai, Lord, 190, 191

Matsudaira Gettan, Lord, 190, 191

Matthew, Gospel of, 193

meibutsu: The Tea utensils chosen before the time of Sen no Rikyū are referred to as *ō-meibutsu* ("Great Masterpieces"); those chosen by Rikyū as *meibutsu;* those chosen after the time of Rikyū (i.e., by Kobori Enshū), as *chūkō-meibutsu,* 180, 185, 190, 195, 212, 213

Meiji period (1868-1912), 91, 103, 104, 162, 191

Mencius, 188

Ming dynasty, 120, 159, 202

mingei, 95

Mingei-kai, 94

Mishima: Korean ware inlaid or brushmarked with white slip, 172-74, 99

Mokubei (1783-1855): Kyoto potter, painter, poet, and scholar, 198

Mokujiki Shōnin (1536-1608): Itinerant Buddhist priest and sculptor, 98, *Pl.41*

Morris, William, 90, 91, 94, 107

mu: "Nothingness"; beyond nothing and something, 114, 124

muge: "No-hindrance"; egoless state where all obstructions cease, 129, 130

Murata Shukō (1421-1502): The Tea master who initiated the Way of Tea, 212

mushin: "No Mind"; state of going beyond all forms of dualism, 112

music, Okinawan, 164

musō: "No Form", 121

Nabeshima ware, 198

Naeshirogawa ware, 169, *Pl. 55*

Naha, 158, 161, 163

Nakamura Sosetsu, 190

Nan-ch'üan P'u-yüan (748-834): T'ang dynasty Zen master, 139

nanga: Chinese painting of the "Southern School" and its Japanese derivative, 120, 149

nangyō-dō: the "Way of Hardship", 132

Nan-yüeh Huai-jang (d. 775): T'ang dynasty Zen master, 145

Nō drama, 164, 165, 181

Ohara, Magosaburō, 102

Okakura, Kakuzō, 120, 121

Okinawa, 158-70

Ōshima-gasuri; kasuri made on Amami Ōshima island, 168

painting, 116, 118, 120, 145, 148, 218, *Pls. 5, 11, 29, 42*

Perry, Commodore, 91

Persian rugs, 200

Peruvian textiles, 223

Picasso, Pablo, 119
Plotinus, 146
pottery, 118, 120-22, 124, 125, 129, 198, 199, 218, 219, *Pls. 6, 9, 10, 32, 55, 56, 68, 76*
  English, *Pls. 20, 21, 36*
  Inuyama, 169
  Korean, 121, 122, 132, 139, 142, 143, 171-76, 190-96, 199, *Pls. 1, 3, 4, 38, 57, 59, 64-67*
  Mishima, 199
  Nabeshima, 198
  Naeshirogawa, 169, *Pl. 55*
  Okinawan, 162, 163, 169, 170, *Pls. 51-54*
  Sung, 121, 131-35, 147, 170, 220-23, *Pl. 22*
  Swankolok, *Pl. 28*
Pre-Raphaelite painters, 90
Pure Land Buddhism, 142

Raku Tea-bowls, 120, 121, 125, 126, 195
Raku Chōjirō, 194
Religio Medici, 140
Rembrandt, 93
Representative Men, 222
rugs, 118, 200
Ruskin, John, 90
Ryūkyū Islands, 103, 118, 158-70

sabi, 123
Sangatsu-dō, Nara, 163
Satsuma-jōfu: Hemp *kasuri* from Okinawa and Kagoshima Prefecture, 168
sculpture, 148, 218, *Pls. 14, 15, 41*
Sen no Rikyū, 151, 212
shibui, 123, 124, 147, 183, 184, 213, 214
Shirakaba, 93, 94
Shuri, Okinawa, 161, 162, 167, 168, *Pls. 43, 45-47*
Skansen Folk Museum, 102
Sōami, 212
Socrates, 217
soku: The relationship in which the particular implies and equates with Unity, 144
Songs of Innocence, 141
St. Ives, Cornwall, 94
St. Francis of Assisi, 149
St. Paul, 214

Sung dynasty, 121, 131-35, 147, 170, 208, 215, 220-23
Suzuki, Dr. Daisetsu, 10, 87, 99

Taiwan, 158, 159, 168
Takeda Kizaemon, 190
Takeno Jōō, 151, 212
tariki: "Other Strength"; the reliance on grace, 10, 125, 132, 133, 204, 215
Tawaraya Sōtatsu, 112
Tea, Way of, 88, 91, 98, 120, 121, 123-26, 147-51, 170, 177-89, 190, 193, 212, 213, 219
Tea-bowls, 121, 123, 125, 126, 149, 150, 151, 190-96
Tea-gardens, 186, 188
Tea-rooms, 122, 186, 188, 212, 213
textiles, *Pls. 26, 31, 39, 72*
   Coptic, 136, 223, *Pl. 27*
   Peruvian, 223
   Ryūkyū, 103, 118, 166-69, *Pls. 2, 7, 30, 50*
Theologia Germanica, 153
tiles, roof, 162, 163
Tokugawa Mausoleum, Nikkō, 161
Tokugawa shogunate, 91, 104
tombs, 159-61, *Pls. 43, 44*
Tomimoto, Kenkichi, 98
Toshi Ieshige, 190
Tōshōdai-ji temple, Nara, 163
Tsuboya, Okinawa, 169, 170
Tz'u-chou, 134, 135

United States of America, 96, 107, 120, 217, 218

wabi, 123, 184
weaving, 118, 145
  Okinawan, 167, 168
  tapestry, 206
Whitman, Walt, 93
woodwork, Gothic, 199

Yaeyama Island, 164
Yamamoto, Tamesaburō, 102
Yi dynasty, 97, 98, 101, 121, 142, 143
Yūzen dyeing: Technique employing paste and hand painting, 166, 167

Zen, 10, 112, 114, 123-25, 129, 137-40, 144, 145, 147, 150, 156, 157, 164, **175,** 188, 193, 196, 201, 204, 215

The Author: Sōetsu Yanagi was born in Tokyo in 1889 and graduated from the literature department of the Tokyo Imperial University in 1913, majoring in psychology. Proficient in English and with a deep feeling for art, while still a student Mr. Yanagi became associated with the *Shirakaba* ("Silver Birch") literary group, to which he was partly responsible for interpreting Western art to Japan.

In 1921, he completed the organization of a Korean folkcraft museum in Seoul, and, in 1936, the present Japan Folkcraft Museum in Tokyo was completed through his efforts.

Mr. Yanagi travelled widely in the Orient, Europe, and America. In 1929 he lectured at Harvard University for one year. In Japan, sometimes in the company of the potters Kanjirō Kawai, Shōji Hamada, and Bernard Leach, he sought out anonymous craftsman of all kinds throughout the country and encouraged their work. He also wrote prolifically and profoundly on all aspects of aesthetics, finding his inspiration in Japanese and Oriental folkcraft and folk culture. His personal collection of folkcrafts is the nucleus of the Japan Folkcraft Museum collection. Mr. Yanagi died in Tokyo in 1961.

The Adaptor: Bernard Leach today is known as one of the world's greatest potters. His numerous books are familiar to everyone interested in modern crafts. Mr. Leach first came to Japan at the age of 22, in 1909, met the *Shirakaba* group and soon became an intimate friend of Sōetsu Yanagi. It is difficult to say which of the two men influenced the other the more. In Mr. Yanagi's own words, "Leach came to Japan . . . full of dreams and wonder. . . . It is doubtful if any other visitor from the West ever shared our spiritual life so completely". This volume is Mr. Leach's tribute to his friend of fifty years standing.